ANIMALS' RIGHTS

"I saw deep in the eyes of the animals the human soul look out upon me.

"I saw where it was born deep down under feathers and fur, or condemned for awhile to roam four-footed among the brambles. I caught the clinging mute glance of the prisoner, and swore that I would be faithful.

"Thee my brother and sister I see and mistake not. Do not be afraid. Dwelling thus for a while, fulfilling thy appointed time—thou too shalt come to thyself at last.

"Thy half-warm horns and long tongue lapping round my wrist do not conceal thy humanity any more than the learned talk of the pedant conceals his—for all thou art dumb we have words and plenty between us.

"Come nigh, little bird, with your half-stretched quivering wings—within you I behold choirs of angels, and the Lord himself in vista."

Towards Democracy.

ANIMALS' RIGHTS
Considered in Relation to Social Progress

by
HENRY S. SALT
Author of *The Life of Henry David Thoreau*

Preface by Peter Singer

CENTAUR PRESS LIMITED
London

Copyright © 1980 by Society for Animal Rights, Inc. All rights reserved. Printed in the United States of America.

First published in Great Britain 1980 by Centaur Press Ltd., Fontwell Sussex and 11-14 Stanhope Mews West, London, S W 7

ISBN   0 90000098 8

PREFACE

HENRY SALT was born in 1851 and died in 1939. It would be true to say that he is now almost totally forgotten, except that this implies that he was once well known, which he was not. Yet he was a remarkable person. He wrote nearly forty books, most of them urging humane reforms in prison conditions, schools, in the economic organization of society, and in the treatment of animals. His opinion of his fellow-countrymen, as well as his dry, ironical wit, are both epitomized by the title he gave to the story of his life in England: *Seventy Years Among Savages*. Though educated at Eton and Cambridge, Salt lived very frugally in a country cottage, growing his own vegetables and drawing to himself such visitors as George Bernard Shaw, William Morris, G. K. Chesterton, the Labour Party leader H. M. Hyndman, Sidney and Beatrice Webb, Ramsay MacDonald—later to be the first Labour Prime Minister of Britain—and Havelock Ellis, whose writings on sex were among the first to break

Victorian taboos and discuss the issue openly.

Salt's ideas often reached the public through his friends, rather than in his own name. Shaw once wrote: "My pastime has been writing sermons in plays, sermons preaching what Salt practised." More momentous still was his influence on Gandhi, whom Salt had befriended when Gandhi first arrived in England, alone, unknown and unable to find vegetarian food. Gandhi later wrote that he owed his thoughts about civil disobedience and non-cooperation to Salt's book on the then little-known American radical, Henry Thoreau. (Gandhi's example in turn inspired Martin Luther King, and thus Thoreau's ideas returned to the land of their origin.)

We have now caught up with some of Salt's ideas. We no longer flog schoolchildren. The barbarism of prison life has been softened a little. But we have not caught up with *Animals' Rights*. We still raise animals which are, as Salt put it, "scarcely more than animated beef or mutton or pork." Fashions having changed, we no longer slaughter vast numbers of birds to put feathers in ladies' hats, as Salt describes; but the fur trade, no less wanton a waste of animal life, continues to prosper and grow. As Salt anticipated, the advance of mechanization has released horses from their role as beasts of burden; but it has also meant the industrialization of farming, which confines animals in small cages and denies them what Salt regarded as their fundamental right: the right to live a natural life, a life permitting individual development. And if Salt was concerned about animal experiments in 1892, when they numbered in the thousands, what would he have thought of today's total of 5½ million experiments each year in Britain, and 60 to 100 million in the United States?

Animals' Rights was not the first book to defend the case for the rights of animals, as Salt's own excellent bibliography makes clear. The essential argument—that if all human beings are equal, there is no reason to deny equality to "the brutes" as well—was sketched by Thomas Taylor in his anonymous *Vindication of the Rights of Brutes*, published in 1792. But Taylor's purpose was to ridicule the idea of equal rights for humans rather than to uphold the rights of animals. In the century that passed between Taylor's book and Salt's, several authors used the same argument in favour of animals rather than against humans. Jeremy Bentham argued that there is no "insuperable line" dividing humans from animals, and the latter must be given the protection of legal rights, as the former are. John Lawrence, in his *Philosophical Treatise on Horses and on The Moral Duties of Man towards the Brute*

Creation argued that because animals have life, intelligence and feeling, they must have rights; and the argument was repeated, with variations, by Thomas Young, Lewis Gompertz and Edward Nicholson.

Though not the first, *Animals' Rights* is, I believe, the best of the eighteenth- and nineteenth-century works on the rights of animals. Every time I re-read Salt's book—and I have now read it several times—I marvel at how he anticipates almost every point discussed in the contemporary debate over animal rights. Defenders of animals, myself included, have been able to add relatively little to the essential case Salt outlined in 1892; but we can console ourselves with the fact that our opponents have been able to come up with few objections that Salt has not already dealt with. That one species preying on another is natural and therefore right; that animals are radically different from humans and have no soul, or no emotional life; that wild animals benefit by our taming and capturing them; that the consumption of animal flesh is somehow necessary; that because we are responsible for bringing domestic animals into existence we may do as we please with them; and that we may eat animals with a clear conscience because the Bible gives us permission to do

Preface

so—all of these arguments, even the last, are still used to justify our abuse of animals. *Animals' Rights* is of more than merely historical interest: it remains a living contribution to a continuing debate.

Of course, the very fact that the debate over animals has progressed so little since Salt forces us to acknowledge that for all Salt's arguments, his learning, his manifest humanitarian feeling and his fine sense of humour, *Animals' Rights* failed to alter public opinion or practice. The book, originally published in both New York and London, was reprinted in America two years later, with an "Essay on Vivisection" by Albert Leffingwell as an appendix; it reappeared in a revised edition in London in 1905 and was again revised in 1922; but it had no real impact outside humanitarian and vegetarian circles. For progressive thinkers the issue was an unfashionable one, while Establishment figures, if they heard of it at all, ignored it. Among academic philosophers, only D. G. Ritchie discussed it, in his *Natural Rights*, published in 1894—and Ritchie was critical. (Salt replied to his objections in an appendix to the next edition of *Animals' Rights*.) After that the issue faded away and was not heard of again until the early 1970s, when human rights for blacks and women were a major political issue and the extension of the argument to nonhuman animals again seemed a logical short step.

We now find ourselves at a stage in the development of concern for nonhuman animals when there is a sufficiently large interested audience to justify making *Animals' Rights* available again, after an interval of fifty years. When the book was written, it was far ahead of its time. Whether its time has yet come remains to be seen.

Peter Singer

Melbourne, Australia
March 1980

PREFATORY NOTE

THE object of the following essay is to set the principle of animals' rights on a consistent and intelligible footing, to show that this principle underlies the various efforts of humanitarian reformers, and to make a clearance of the comfortable fallacies which the apologists of the present system have industriously accumulated. While not hesitating to speak strongly when occasion demanded, I have tried to avoid the tone of irrelevant recrimination so common in these controversies, and thus to give more unmistakable emphasis to the vital points at issue. We have to decide, not whether the practice of fox-hunting, for example, is more, or less, cruel than vivisection, but whether *all* practices which inflict unnecessary pain on sentient beings are not incompatible with the higher instincts of humanity.

I am aware that many of my contentions

will appear very ridiculous to those who view the subject from a contrary standpoint, and regard the lower animals as created solely for the pleasure and advantage of man; on the other hand, I have myself derived an unfailing fund of amusement from a rather extensive study of our adversaries' reasoning. It is a conflict of opinion, wherein time alone can adjudicate; but already there are not a few signs that the laugh will rest ultimately with the humanitarians.

My thanks are due to several friends who have helped me in the preparation of this book; I may mention Mr. Ernest Bell, Mr. Kenneth Romanes, and Mr. W. E. A. Axon. My many obligations to previous writers are acknowledged in the footnotes and appendices.

H. S. S.

September, 1892.

CONTENTS

CHAPTER I. THE PRINCIPLE OF ANIMALS' RIGHTS.

The general doctrine of rights; Herbert Spencer's definition. Early advocates of animals' rights; "Martin's Act," 1822. Need of an intelligible principle. Two main causes of the denial of animals' rights; (1) The "religious" notion that animals have no souls, (2) the Cartesian theory that animals have no consciousness. The individuality of animals. Opinions of Schopenhauer, Darwin, etc. The question of nomenclature; objectionable use of such terms as "brute-beast," etc. The progressiveness of humanitarian feeling; analogous instance of negro-slavery. Difficulties and objections; arguments drawn from "the struggle of life." Animals' rights not antagonistic to human rights. Summary of the principle . . . . . . pp. 1-29

CHAPTER II. THE CASE OF DOMESTIC ANIMALS.

Special claims of the domestic animals; services performed by them; human obligations in return. Opinions of Humphry Primatt and John Lawrence. Common disregard of rights in the case of horses, cattle, sheep, etc. Castration of animals. Treat-

ment of dogs and cats. Condition of the household "pet" compared with that of the "beast of burden."
pp. 30-44

CHAPTER III. THE CASE OF WILD ANIMALS.

Wild animals have rights, though not yet recognized in law. The influence of property. Man not justified in injuring any harmless animal. The condition of animals in menageries; the fallacy that "they gain by it." Caged birds. A right relationship must be based on sympathy not power   pp. 45-53

CHAPTER IV. THE SLAUGHTER OF ANIMALS FOR FOOD.

Important bearing of the food question on the consideration of animals' rights. The assumption that flesh-food is necessary; contradictory statements of flesh-eaters. Experience proves that man is not compelled to kill animals for food. Cruelties inseparable from slaughtering; feeling of repugnance thereby aroused. The logic of these facts. Ingenious attempts at evasion: "Animals would otherwise not exist;" "scriptural permission." The coming success of food-reform . .   pp. 54-66

CHAPTER V. SPORT, OR AMATEUR BUTCHERY.

Sport the most wanton of all violations of animals' rights. Childish fallacies of sportsmen. Tame stag hunting; rabbit-coursing; cruel treatment of "vermin;" steel traps. The testimony of an expert on cover-shooting . . . .   pp. 67-78

Contents

CHAPTER VI. MURDEROUS MILLINERY.

The fur and feather traffic. In what sense it is "necessary;" the use of leather. Fashionable demand for furs causes whole provinces to be ransacked. The wearing of feathers in bonnets; heartless massacre of birds. Due to ignorance and thoughtlessness.
pp. 79-89

CHAPTER VII. EXPERIMENTAL TORTURE.

The analytical methods of scientists and naturalists. Vivisection the logical outcome of this mood. The horrors of vivisection. Its alleged utility. Moral considerations involved; nothing that is inhuman can be in accord with true science. Experiments on animals as compared with experiments on men. The plea that vivisection is "no worse" than other cruelties. The exact significance of vivisection in the question of animals' rights . . pp. 90-103

CHAPTER VIII. LINES OF REFORM.

The lesson of the foregoing instances of cruelty and injustice; the only solution of the problem is to recognize animals' rights. No "sentimentality," where difficulties are fairly faced. The future path of humanitarianism. Human interests involved in animals' rights; extension of the idea of "humanity" both in western thought and oriental tradition. The movement essentially a democratic one; the emancipation of man will bring with it the emancipation of animals. Practical steps toward securing the rights of animals: (1) Education. Useless to preach humanity to children only; need of an intellectual and literary crusade. The laugh to be turned against the real sentimentalists, our opponents. (2) Legislation. *Laisser-faire* objections refuted. Cases where immediate action is desirable. Conclusion.

pp. 104-131

APPENDIX

The term "rights." Bibliography. An updated bibliography—books, philosophical journal articles, and essays, selections, articles, discussions, reviews, etc. Works by Henry S. Salt; works edited by Henry S. Salt. Biographical notes. . . . . . pp. 133-231

ANIMALS' RIGHTS

CHAPTER I

THE PRINCIPLE OF ANIMALS' RIGHTS

HAVE the lower animals "rights?" Undoubtedly—if men have. That is the point I wish to make evident in this opening chapter. But have men rights? Let it be stated at the outset that I have no intention of discussing the abstract theory of natural rights, which, at the present time, is looked upon with suspicion and disfavour by many social reformers, since it has not unfrequently been made to cover the most extravagant and contradictory assertions. But though its phraseology is confessedly vague and perilous, there is nevertheless a solid truth underlying it—a truth which has always been clearly apprehended by the moral faculty, however difficult it may be to establish it on an unassailable logical basis. If men have not "rights"—well, they have an unmistakable intimation of something very similar ; a sense of justice which marks the boundary-line where acquiescence ceases and resistance begins ; a demand for freedom to live their own life, subject to the necessity of respecting the equal freedom of other people.

Such is the doctrine of rights as formulated by Herbert Spencer. "Every man," he says, "is free to do that which he wills, provided he infringes not the equal liberty of any other man." And again, "Whoever admits that each man must have a certain restricted freedom, asserts that it is *right* he should have this restricted freedom. . . . And hence the several particular freedoms deducible may fitly be called, as they commonly are called, his *rights*."[1]

The fitness of this nomenclature is disputed, but the existence of some real principle of the kind can hardly be called in question ; so that the controversy concerning "rights" is little else than an academic battle over words, which leads to no practical conclusion. I shall assume, therefore, that men are possessed of "rights," in the sense of Herbert Spencer's

[1] "Justice," pp. 46, 62.

The Principle of Animals' Rights

definition; and if any of my readers object to this qualified use of the term, I can only say that I shall be perfectly willing to change the word as soon as a more appropriate one is forthcoming. The immediate question that claims our attention is this—if men have rights, have animals their rights also?

From the earliest times there have been thinkers who, directly or indirectly, answered this question with an affirmative. The Buddhist and Pythagorean canons, dominated perhaps by the creed of reincarnation, included the maxim "not to kill or injure any innocent animal." The humanitarian philosophers of the Roman empire, among whom Seneca and Plutarch and Porphyry were the most conspicuous, took still higher ground in preaching humanity on the broadest principle of universal benevolence. "Since justice is due to rational beings," wrote Porphyry, "how is it possible to evade the admission that we are bound also to act justly towards the races below us?"

It is a lamentable fact that during the churchdom of the middle ages, from the fourth century to the sixteenth, from the time of Porphyry to the time of Montaigne, little or no attention was paid to the question of the rights and wrongs of the lower races. Then, with the Reformation and the revival of learning, came a revival also of humanitarian feeling, as may be seen in many passages of Erasmus and More, Shakespeare and Bacon; but it was not until the eighteenth century, the age of enlightenment and "sensibility," of which Voltaire and Rousseau were the spokesmen, that the rights of animals obtained more deliberate recognition. From the great Revolution of 1789 dates the period when the world-wide spirit of humanitarianism, which had hitherto been felt by but one man in a million—the thesis of the philosopher or the vision of the poet—began to disclose itself, gradually and dimly at first, as an essential feature of democracy.

A great and far-reaching effect was produced in England at this time by the publication of such revolutionary works as Paine's "Rights of Man," and Mary Wollstonecraft's "Vindication of the Rights of Women;" and looking back now, after the lapse of a hundred years, we can see that a still wider extension of the theory of rights was thenceforth inevitable. In fact, such a claim was anticipated—if only in bitter jest—by a contemporary writer, who furnishes us with a notable

The Principle of Animals' Rights

instance of how the mockery of one generation may become the reality of the next. There was published anonymously in 1792 a little volume entitled "A Vindication of the Rights of Brutes,"[1] a *reductio ad absurdum* of Mary Wollstonecraft's essay, written, as the author informs us, "to evince by demonstrative arguments the perfect equality of what is called the irrational species to the human." The further opinion is expressed that "after those wonderful productions of Mr. Paine and Mrs. Wollstonecraft, such a theory as the present seems to be necessary." It *was* necessary; and a very short term of years sufficed to bring it into effect; indeed, the theory had already been put forward by several English pioneers of nineteenth-century humanitarianism.

To Jeremy Bentham, in particular, belongs the high honour of first asserting the rights of animals with authority and persistence. "The legislator," he wrote, "ought to interdict everything which may serve to lead to cruelty. The barbarous spectacles of gladiators no doubt contributed to give the Romans that ferocity which they displayed in their civil wars. A people accustomed to despise human

[1] Attributed to Thomas Taylor, the Platonist.

life in their games could not be expected to respect it amid the fury of their passions. It is proper for the same reason to forbid every kind of cruelty towards animals, whether by way of amusement, or to gratify gluttony. Cock-fights, bull-baiting, hunting hares and foxes, fishing, and other amusements of the same kind, necessarily suppose either the absence of reflection or a fund of inhumanity, since they produce the most acute sufferings to sensible beings, and the most painful and lingering death of which we can form any idea. Why should the law refuse its protection to any sensitive being? The time will come when humanity will extend its mantle over everything which breathes. We have begun by attending to the condition of slaves; we shall finish by softening that of all the animals which assist our labours or supply our wants."[1]

So, too, wrote one of Bentham's contemporaries: "The grand source of the unmerited and superfluous misery of beasts exists in a defect in the constitution of all communities. No human government, I believe, has ever recognized the *jus animalium*, which ought surely to form a part of the jurisprudence of every

[1] "Principles of Penal Law," chap. xvi.

system founded on the principles of justice and humanity."[1] A large number of later moralists have followed on the same lines, with the result that the rights of animals have already, to a certain limited extent, been established both in private usage and by legal enactment.

It is interesting to note the exact commencement of this new principle in law. When Lord Erskine, speaking in the House of Lords in 1811, advocated the cause of justice to the lower animals, he was greeted with loud cries of insult and derision. But eleven years later the efforts of the despised humanitarians, and especially of Richard Martin, of Galway, were rewarded by their first success. The passing of the Ill-treatment of Cattle Bill, commonly known as "Martin's Act," in June, 1822, is a memorable date in the history of humane legislation, less on account of the positive protection afforded by it, for it applied only to cattle and "beasts of burden," than for the invaluable precedent which it created. From 1822 onward, the principle of that *jus animalium* for which Bentham had pleaded, was re-

[1] John Lawrence, "Philosophical Treatise on the Moral Duties of Man towards the Brute Creation," 1796.

cognized, however partially and tentatively at first, by English law, and the animals included in the Act ceased to be the mere property of their owners; moreover the Act has been several times supplemented and extended during the past half century.[1] It is scarcely possible, in the face of this legislation, to maintain that "rights" are a privilege with which none but human beings can be invested; for if *some* animals are already included within the pale of protection, why should not more and more be so included in the future?

For the present, however, what is most urgently needed is some comprehensive and intelligible principle, which shall indicate, in a more consistent manner, the true lines of man's moral relation towards the lower animals. And here, it must be admitted, our position is still far from satisfactory; for though certain very important concessions have been made, as we have seen, to the demand for the *jus animalium*, they have been made for the most part in a grudging, unwilling spirit, and rather in the interests of *property* than of *principle;* while even the leading advocates of animals'

[1] Viz.: in 1833, 1835, 1849, 1854, 1876, 1884. We shall have occasion, in subsequent chapters, to refer to some of these enactments.

rights seem to have shrunk from basing their claim on the only argument which can ultimately be held to be a really sufficient one—the assertion that animals, as well as men, though, of course, to a far less extent than men, are possessed of a distinctive individuality, and, therefore, are in justice entitled to live their lives with a due measure of that "restricted freedom" to which Herbert Spencer alludes. It is of little use to claim "rights" for animals in a vague general way, if with the same breath we explicitly show our determination to subordinate those rights to anything and everything that can be construed into a human "want;" nor will it ever be possible to obtain full justice for the lower races so long as we continue to regard them as beings of a wholly different order, and to ignore the significance of their numberless points of kinship with mankind.

For example, it has been said by a well-known writer on the subject of humanity to animals [1] that "the life of a brute, having no moral purpose, can best be understood ethically as representing the sum of its *pleasures;* and the obligation, therefore, of producing the

[1] "Fraser," November, 1863; "The Rights of Man and the Claims of Brutes."

pleasures of sentient creatures must be reduced, in their case, to the abstinence from unnecessary destruction of life." Now, with respect to this statement, I must say that the notion of the life of an animal having "no moral purpose," belongs to a class of ideas which cannot possibly be accepted by the advanced humanitarian thought of the present day—it is a purely arbitrary assumption, at variance with our best instincts, at variance with our best science, and absolutely fatal (if the subject be clearly thought out) to any full realization of animals' rights. If we are ever going to do justice to the lower races, we must get rid of the antiquated notion of a "great gulf" fixed between them and mankind, and must recognize the common bond of humanity that unites all living beings in one universal brotherhood.

As far as any excuses can be alleged, in explanation of the insensibility or inhumanity of the western nations in their treatment of animals, these excuses may be mostly traced back to one or the other of two theoretical contentions, wholly different in origin, yet alike in this—that both postulate an absolute difference of nature between men and the lower kinds.

The first is the so-called "religious" notion,

which awards immortality to man, but to man alone, thereby furnishing (especially in Catholic countries) a quibbling justification for acts of cruelty to animals, on the plea that they " have no souls." " It should seem," says a modern writer,[1] " as if the primitive Christians, by laying so much stress upon a future life, in contradistinction to *this* life, and placing the lower creatures out of the pale of hope, placed them at the same time out of the pale of sympathy, and thus laid the foundation for this utter disregard of animals in the light of our fellow-creatures."

I am aware that a quite contrary argument has, in a few isolated instances, been founded on the belief that animals have "no souls." Humphry Primatt, for example, says that " cruelty to a brute is an injury irreparable," because there is no future life to be a compensation for present afflictions; and there is an amusing story, told by Lecky in his " History of European Morals," of a certain humanely-minded Cardinal, who used to allow vermin to bite him without hindrance, on the ground that " *we* shall have heaven to reward us for our sufferings, but these poor creatures

[1] Mrs. Jameson, " Book of Thoughts, Memories, and Fancies," 1854.

have nothing but the enjoyment of this present life." But this is a rare view of the question which need not, I think, be taken into very serious account; for, on the whole, the denial of immortality to animals (unless, of course, it be also denied to men) tends strongly to lessen their chance of being justly and considerately treated. Among the many humane movements of the present age, none is more significant than the growing inclination, noticeable both in scientific circles and in religious, to believe that mankind and the lower animals have the same destiny before them, whether that destiny be for immortality or for annihilation.[1]

The second and not less fruitful source of modern inhumanity is to be found in the "Cartesian" doctrine — the theory of Descartes and his followers — that the lower animals are devoid of consciousness and feeling; a theory which carried the "religious" notion a step further, and deprived the

---

[1] See the article on "Animal Immortality," "The Nineteenth Century," Jan., 1891, by Norman Pearson. The upshot of his argument is, that "if we accept the immortality of the human soul, and *also* accept its evolutional origin, we cannot deny the survival, in some form or other, of animal minds."

The Principle of Animals' Rights

animals not only of their claim to a life hereafter, but of anything that could, without mockery, be called a life in the present, since mere "animated machines," as they were thus affirmed to be, could in no real sense be said to *live* at all! Well might Voltaire turn his humane ridicule against this most monstrous contention, and suggest, with scathing irony, that God " had given the animals the organs of feeling, to the end that they might *not* feel!" " The theory of animal automatism," says one of the leading scientists of the present day,[1] " which is usually attributed to Descartes, can never be accepted by common sense." Yet it is to be feared that it has done much, in its time, to harden " scientific " sense against the just complaints of the victims of human arrogance and oppression.

Let me here quote a most impressive passage from Schopenhauer. " The unpardonable forgetfulness in which the lower animals have hitherto been left by the moralists of

---

[1] G. J. Romanes, "Animal Intelligence." Prof. Huxley's remarks, in " Science and Culture," give a partial support to Descartes' theory, but do not bear on the moral question of rights. For, though he concludes that animals are probably " sensitive automata," he classes men in the same category.

Europe is well known. It is pretended that the beasts have no rights. They persuade themselves that our conduct in regard to them has nothing to do with morals, or (to speak the language of their morality) that we have no duties towards animals: a doctrine revolting, gross, and barbarous, peculiar to the west, and having its root in Judaism. In philosophy, however, it is made to rest upon a hypothesis, admitted, in despite of evidence itself, of an absolute difference between man and beast. It is Descartes who has proclaimed it in the clearest and most decisive manner; and in fact it was a necessary consequence of his errors. The Cartesian-Leibnitzian-Wolfian philosophy, with the assistance of entirely abstract notions, had built up the 'rational psychology,' and constructed an immortal *anima rationalis:* but, visibly, the world of beasts, with its very natural claims, stood up against this exclusive monopoly—this *brevet* of immortality decreed to man alone—and silently Nature did what she always does in such cases—she protested. Our philosophers, feeling their scientific conscience quite disturbed, were forced to attempt to consolidate their 'rational psychology' by the aid of empiricism. They therefore set themselves to

The Principle of Animals' Rights

work to hollow out between man and beast an enormous abyss, of an immeasurable width; by this they wish to prove to us, in contempt of evidence, an impassable difference."[1]

The fallacious idea that the lives of animals have "no moral purpose" is at root connected with these religious and philosophical pretensions which Schopenhauer so powerfully condemns. To live one's own life—to realize one's true self—is the highest moral purpose of man and animal alike; and that animals possess their due measure of this sense of individuality is scarcely open to doubt. "We have seen," says Darwin, "that the senses and intuitions, the various emotions and faculties, such as love, memory, attention, curiosity, imitation, reason, etc., of which man boasts, may be found in an incipient, or even sometimes in a well-developed condition, in the lower animals."[2] Not less emphatic is the testimony of the Rev. J. G. Wood, who, speaking from a great experience, gives it as his opinion that "the manner in which we ignore individuality in the lower animals is

[1] Schopenhauer's "Foundation of Morality." I quote the passage as translated in Mr. Howard Williams's "Ethics of Diet."
[2] "Descent of Man," chap. iii.

simply astounding." He claims for them a future life, because he is "quite sure that most of the cruelties which are perpetrated on the animals are due to the habit of considering them as mere machines without susceptibilities, without reason, and without the capacity of a future."[1]

This, then, is the position of those who assert that animals, like men, are necessarily possessed of certain limited rights, which cannot be withheld from them as they are now withheld without tyranny and injustice. They have individuality, character, reason; and to have those qualities is to have the right to exercise them, in so far as surrounding circumstances permit. "Freedom of choice and act," says Ouida, "is the first condition of animal as of human happiness. How many animals in a million have even relative freedom in any moment of their lives? No choice is ever permitted to them; and all their most natural instincts are denied or made subject to authority."[2] Yet no human being is justified in regarding any animal whatsoever as a meaningless automaton, to be worked, or tortured, or eaten, as the case may be, for the

[1] "Man and Beast, here and hereafter," 1874.
[2] "Fortnightly Review," April, 1892.

mere object of satisfying the wants or whims of mankind. Together with the destinies and duties that are laid on them and fulfilled by them, animals have also the right to be treated with gentleness and consideration, and the man who does not so treat them, however great his learning or influence may be, is, in that respect, an ignorant and foolish man, devoid of the highest and noblest culture of which the human mind is capable.

Something must here be said on the important subject of nomenclature. It is to be feared that the ill-treatment of animals is largely due—or at any rate the difficulty of amending that treatment is largely increased —by the common use of such terms as "brute-beast," "live-stock," etc., which implicitly deny to the lower races that intelligent individuality which is most undoubtedly possessed by them. It was long ago remarked by Bentham, in his "Introduction to Principles of Morals and Legislation," that, whereas human beings are styled *persons*, "other animals, on account of their interests having been neglected by the insensibility of the ancient jurists, stand degraded into the class of *things;*" and Schopenhauer also has commented on the mischievous absurdity of the idiom which applies the neuter pronoun "it" to such highly organized primates as the dog and the ape.

A word of protest is needed also against such an expression as "dumb animals," which, though often cited as "an immense exhortation to pity,"[1] has in reality a tendency to influence ordinary people in quite the contrary direction, inasmuch as it fosters the idea of an impassable barrier between mankind and their dependents. It is convenient to us men to be deaf to the entreaties of the victims of our injustice; and, by a sort of grim irony, we therefore assume that it is *they* who are afflicted by some organic incapacity—they are "dumb animals," forsooth! although a moment's consideration must prove that they have innumerable ways, often quite human in variety and suggestiveness, of uttering their thoughts and emotions.[2] Even the term "animals,"

---

[1] In Sir A. Helps's "Animals and their Masters."

[2] Let those who think that men are likely to treat animals with more humanity on account of their dumbness ponder the case of the fish, as exemplified in the following whimsically suggestive passage of Leigh Hunt's "Imaginary Conversations of Pope and Swift." "The Dean once asked a scrub who was fishing, if he had ever caught a fish called the Scream. The man protested that he had never heard of such a fish. 'What!' says the Dean, 'you an angler, and never

as applied to the lower races, is incorrect, and not wholly unobjectionable, since it ignores the fact that *man* is an animal no less than they. My only excuse for using it in this volume is that there is absolutely no other brief term available.

So anomalous is the attitude of man towards the lower animals, that it is no marvel if many humane thinkers have wellnigh despaired over this question. "The whole subject of the brute creation," wrote Dr. Arnold, " is to me one of such painful mystery, that I dare not approach it;" and this (to put the most charitable interpretation on their silence) appears to be the position of the majority of moralists and teachers at the present time. Yet there is urgent need of some key to the solution of the problem ; and in no other way can this key be found than by the full inclusion of the lower races within the pale of human sympathy. All the promptings of our best and

heard of the fish that gives a shriek when coming out of the water ? 'Tis the only fish that has a voice, and a sad, dismal sound it is.' The man asked who could be so barbarous as to angle for a creature that shrieked. 'That,' said the Dean, 'is another matter ; but what do you think of fellows that I have seen, whose only reason for hooking and tearing all the fish they can get at, is that they do *not* scream ? "

surest instincts point us in this direction. "It is abundantly evident," says Lecky,[1] "both from history and from present experience, that the instinctive shock, or natural feelings of disgust, caused by the sight of the sufferings of men, is not generically different from that which is caused by the sight of the suffering of animals."

If this be so—and the admission is a momentous one—can it be seriously contended that the same humanitarian tendency which has already emancipated the slave, will not ultimately benefit the lower races also? Here, again, the historian of "European Morals" has a significant remark: "At one time," he says, "the benevolent affections embrace merely the family, soon the circle expanding includes first a class, then a nation, then a coalition of nations, then all humanity; and finally its influence is felt in the dealings of man with the animal world. In each of these cases a standard is formed, different from that of the preceding stage, but in each case the same tendency is recognized as virtue."[2]

But, it may be argued, vague sympathy with the lower animals is one thing, and a definite

---

[1] "History of European Morals."
[2] *Ibid.* i. 101.

The Principle of Animals' Rights

recognition of their "rights" is another; what reason is there to suppose that we shall advance from the former phase to the latter? Just this; that every great liberating movement has proceeded exactly on these lines. Oppression and cruelty are invariably founded on a lack of imaginative sympathy; the tyrant or tormentor can have no true sense of kinship with the victim of his injustice. When once the sense of affinity is awakened, the knell of tyranny is sounded, and the ultimate concession of "rights" is simply a matter of time. The present condition of the more highly organized domestic animals is in many ways very analogous to that of the negro slaves of a hundred years ago: look back, and you will find in their case precisely the same exclusion from the common pale of humanity; the same hypocritical fallacies, to justify that exclusion; and, as a consequence, the same deliberate stubborn denial of their social "rights." Look back—for it is well to do so—and then look forward, and the moral can hardly be mistaken.

We find so great a thinker and writer as Aristotle seriously pondering whether a slave may be considered as in any sense a *man.* In emphasizing the point that friendship is founded on propinquity, he expresses himself as follows:

"Neither can men have friendships with horses, cattle, or slaves, considered merely as such; for a slave is merely a living instrument, and an instrument a living slave. Yet, considered as a man, a slave may be an object of friendship, for certain rights seem to belong to all those capable of participating in law and engagement. A slave, then, considered as a man, may be treated justly or unjustly."[1] "Slaves," says Bentham, "have been treated by the law exactly upon the same footing as in England, for example, the inferior races of animals are still. The day *may* come when the rest of the animal creation may acquire those rights which could never have been withholden from them but by the hand of tyranny."[2]

Let us unreservedly admit the immense difficulties that stand in the way of this animal enfranchisement. Our relation towards the animals is complicated and embittered by innumerable habits handed down through centuries of mistrust and brutality; we cannot, in all cases, suddenly relax these habits, or do full justice even where we see that justice will have to be done. A perfect ethic of

[1] "Ethics," book viii.
[2] "Principles of Morals and Legislation."

humaneness is therefore impracticable, if not unthinkable; and we can attempt to do no more than to indicate in a general way the main principle of animals' rights, noting at the same time the most flagrant particular violations of those rights, and the lines on which the only valid reform can hereafter be effected. But, on the other hand, it may be remembered, for the comfort and encouragement of humanitarian workers, that these obstacles are, after all, only such as are inevitable in each branch of social improvement; for at every stage of every great reformation it has been repeatedly argued, by indifferent or hostile observers, that further progress is impossible; indeed, when the opponents of a great cause begin to demonstrate its "impossibility," experience teaches us that that cause is already on the high road to fulfilment.

As for the demand so frequently made on reformers, that they should first explain the details of their scheme—how this and that point will be arranged, and by what process all kinds of difficulties, real or imagined, will be circumvented—the only rational reply is that it is absurd to expect to see the end of a question, when we are now but at its beginning. The persons who offer this futile sort of criticism are usually those who under no circumstances would be open to conviction; they purposely ask for an explanation which, by the very nature of the case, is impossible because it necessarily belongs to a later period of time. It would be equally sensible to request a traveller to enumerate beforehand all the particular things he will see by the way, on pain of being denounced as an unpractical visionary, although he may have a quite sufficient general knowledge of his course and destination.

Our main principle is now clear. If "rights" exist at all—and both feeling and usage indubitably prove that they do exist—they cannot be consistently awarded to men and denied to animals, since the same sense of justice and compassion apply in both cases. "Pain is pain," says an honest old writer,[1] "whether it be inflicted on man or on beast; and the creature that suffers it, whether man or beast, being sensible of the misery of it while it lasts, suffers *evil;* and the sufferance of evil, unmeritedly, unprovokedly, where no offence has been given, and no good can possibly be answered by it, but merely to exhibit

[1] Humphry Primatt, D.D., author of "The Duty of Mercy to Brute Animals" (1776).

power or gratify malice, is Cruelty and Injustice in him that occasions it."

I commend this outspoken utterance to the attention of those ingenious moralists who quibble about the "discipline" of suffering, and deprecate immediate attempts to redress what, it is alleged, may be a necessary instrument for the attainment of human welfare. It is, perhaps, a mere coincidence, but it has been observed that those who are most forward to disallow the rights of others, and to argue that suffering and subjection are the natural lot of all living things, are usually themselves exempt from the operation of this beneficent law, and that the beauty of self-sacrifice is most loudly belauded by those who profit most largely at the expense of their fellow-creatures.

But "nature is one with rapine," say some, and this utopian theory of "rights," if too widely extended, must come in conflict with that iron rule of internecine competition, by which the universe is regulated. But is the universe so regulated? We note that this very objection, which was confidently relied on a few years back by many opponents of the emancipation of the working-classes, is not heard of in that connection now! Our learned economists and men of science, who set themselves to play the defenders of the social *status quo,* have seen their own weapons of " natural selection, "survival of the fittest," and what not, snatched from their hands and turned against them, and are therefore beginning to explain to us, in a scientific manner, what we untutored humanitarians had previously felt to be true, viz., that competition is not by any means the sole governing law among the human race. We are not greatly dismayed, then, to find the same old bugbear trotted out as an argument against animals' rights—indeed, we see already unmistakable signs of a similar complete reversal of the scientific judgment.[1]

[1] See Prince Kropotkine's articles on " Mutual Aid among Animals," "Nineteenth Century," 1890, where the conclusion is arrived at that "sociability is as much a law of nature as mutual struggle." A similar view is expressed in the "Study of Animal Life," 1892, by J. Arthur Thomson. "What we must protest against," he says, in an interesting chapter on "The Struggle of Life," "is that one-sided interpretation according to which individualistic competition is nature's sole method of progress. . . . The precise nature of the means employed and ends attained must be carefully considered when we seek from the records of animal evolution support or justification for human conduct."

The charge of "sentimentalism" is frequently brought against those who plead for animals' rights. Now "sentimentalism," if any meaning at all can be attached to the word, must signify an inequality, an ill balance of sentiment, an inconsistency which leads men into attacking one abuse, while they ignore or condone another where a reform is equally desirable. That this weakness is often observable among "philanthropists" on the one hand, and "friends of animals" on the other, and most of all among those acute "men of the world," whose regard is only for themselves, I am not concerned to deny; what I wish to point out is, that the only real safeguard against sentimentality is to take up a consistent position towards the rights of men and of the lower animals alike, and to cultivate a broad sense of universal justice (not "mercy") for all living things. Herein, and herein alone, is to be sought the true sanity of temperament.

It is an entire mistake to suppose that the rights of animals are in any way antagonistic to the rights of men. Let us not be betrayed for a moment into the specious fallacy that we must study human rights first, and leave the animal question to solve itself hereafter;

for it is only by a wide and disinterested study of *both* subjects that a solution of either is possible. "For he who loves all animated nature," says Porphyry, "will not hate any one tribe of innocent beings, and by how much greater his love for the whole, by so much the more will he cultivate justice towards a part of them, and that part to which he is most allied." To omit all worthier reasons, it is too late in the day to suggest the indefinite postponement of a consideration of animals' rights, for from a moral point of view, and even from a legislative point of view, we are daily confronted with this momentous problem, and the so-called "practical" people who affect to ignore it are simply shutting their eyes to facts which they find it disagreeable to confront.

Once more then, animals have rights, and these rights consist in the "restricted freedom" to live a natural life—a life, that is, which permits of the individual development—subject to the limitations imposed by the permanent needs and interests of the community. There is nothing quixotic or visionary in this assertion; it is perfectly compatible with a readiness to look the sternest laws of existence fully and honestly in the face. If we must kill, whether it be man or animal, let us kill and have done with it; if we must inflict pain, let us do what is inevitable, without hypocrisy, or evasion, or cant. But (here is the cardinal point) let us first be assured that it *is* necessary; let us not wantonly trade on the needless miseries of other beings, and then attempt to lull our consciences by a series of shuffling excuses which cannot endure a moment's candid investigation. As Leigh Hunt well says:

> "That there is pain and evil, is no rule
> That I should make it greater, like a fool."

Thus far of the general principle of animals' rights. We will now proceed to apply this principle to a number of particular cases, from which we may learn something both as to the extent of its present violation, and the possibility of its better observance in the future.

CHAPTER II

THE CASE OF DOMESTIC ANIMALS

THE main principle of animals' rights, if admitted to be fundamentally sound, will not be essentially affected by the wildness or the domesticity, as the case may be, of the animals in question; *both* classes have their rights, though these rights may differ largely in extent and importance. It is convenient, however, to consider the subject of the domestic animals apart from that of the wild ones, inasmuch as their whole relation to mankind is so much altered and emphasized by the fact of their subjection. Here, at any rate, it is impossible, even for the most callous reasoners, to deny the responsibility of man, in his dealings with vast races of beings, the very conditions of whose existence have been modified by human civilization.

An incalculable mass of drudgery, at the cost of incalculable suffering, is daily, hourly performed for the benefit of man by these honest, patient labourers in every town and country of the world. Are these countless services to be permanently ignored in a community which makes any pretension to a humane civilization? Will the free citizens of the enlightened republics of the future be content to reap the immense advantages of animals' labour, without recognizing that they owe them some consideration in return? The question is one that carries with it its own answer. Even now it is nowhere openly contended that domestic animals have no rights.[1]

But the human mind is subtle to evade the full significance of its duties, and nowhere is this more conspicuously seen than in our treatment of the lower races. Given a position in which man profits largely (or *thinks* he profits largely, for it is not always a matter of certainty) by the toil or suffering of the animals, and our respectable moralists are pretty sure to be explaining to us that this providential arrangement is "better for the animals themselves." The wish is father to the thought in

[1] Auguste Comte included the domestic animals as an organic part of the Positivist conception of humanity.

these questions, and there is an accommodating elasticity in our social ethics that permits of the justification of almost any system which it would be inconvenient to us to discontinue. Thus we find it stated, and on the authority of a bishop, that man may "lay down the terms of the social contract between animals and himself," because, forsooth, "the general life of a domestic animal is one of very great comfort—according to the animal's own standard (*sic*) probably one of almost perfect happiness."[1]

Now this prating about "the animal's own standard" is nothing better than hypocritical cant. If man is obliged to lay down the terms of the contract, let him at least do so without having recourse to such a suspiciously opportune afterthought. We have taken the animals from a free, natural state, into an artificial thraldom, in order that *we*, and not *they*, may be the gainers thereby; it cannot possibly be maintained that they owe us gratitude on this account, or that this alleged debt may be used as a means of evading the just recognition of their rights. It is the more necessary to raise a strong protest against this jesuitical

[1] "Moral Duty towards Animals," "Macmillan's Magazine," April, 1882, by the then Bishop of Carlisle.

The Case of Domestic Animals

mode of reasoning, because, as we shall see, it is so frequently employed in one form or another, by the apologists of human tyranny.

On the other hand, I desire to keep clear also of the extreme contrary contention, that man is not morally justified in imposing any sort of subjection on the lower animals.[1] An abstract question of this sort, however interesting as a speculation, and impossible in itself to disprove, is beyond the scope of the present inquiry, which is primarily concerned with the state of things at present existing. We must face the fact that the services of domestic animals have become, whether rightly or wrongly, an integral portion of the system of modern society; we cannot immediately dispense with those services, any more than we can dispense with human labour itself. But we *can* provide, as at least a present step towards a more ideal relationship in the future, that the conditions under which all labour is performed, whether by men or by animals,

---

[1] See Lewis Gompertz' "Moral Inquiries" (1824), where it is argued that "at least in the present state of society it is unjust, and considering the unnecessary abuse they suffer from being in the power of man, it is wrong to use them, and to encourage their being placed in his power."

shall be such as to enable the worker to take some appreciable pleasure in the work, instead of experiencing a lifelong course of injustice and ill-treatment.

And here it may be convenient to say a word as to the existing line of demarcation between the animals legally recognized as "domestic," and those *feræ naturæ*, of wild nature. In the Act of 1849, in which a penalty is imposed for cruelty to "any animal," it is expressly provided that "the word *animal* shall be taken to mean any horse, mare, gelding, bull, ox, cow, heifer, steer, calf, mule, ass, sheep, lamb, hog, pig, sow, goat, dog, cat, or any other domestic animal." It will be shown in a later chapter that the interpretation of this vague reference to "any other" domestic animal is likely to become a point of considerable importance, since it closely affects the welfare of certain animals which, though at present regarded as wild, and therefore outside the pale of protection, are to all intents and purposes in a state of domestication. For the present, however, we may group the domestic animals of this country in three main divisions, (1) horses, asses, and mules; (2) oxen, sheep, goats, and pigs; (3) dogs and cats.

"Food, rest, and tender usage," are declared

by Humphry Primatt, the old author already quoted, to be the three rights of the domestic animals. Lawrence's opinion is to much the same effect. "Man is indispensably bound," he thinks, "to bestow upon animals, in return for the benefit he derives from their services, good and sufficient nourishment, comfortable shelter, and merciful treatment; to commit no wanton outrage upon their feelings, whilst alive, and to put them to the speediest and least painful death, when it shall be necessary to deprive them of life." But it is important to note that something more is due to animals, and especially to domestic animals, than the mere supply of provender and the mere immunity from ill-usage. "We owe justice to men," wrote Montaigne, "and grace and benignity to other creatures that are capable of it; there is a natural commerce and mutual obligation betwixt them and us." Sir Arthur Helps admirably expressed this sentiment in his well-known reference to the duty of "using courtesy to animals."[1]

If these be the rights of domestic animals, it is pitiful to reflect how commonly and how grossly they are violated. The average life of our "beasts of burden," the horse, the ass, and

[1] "Animals and their Masters," p. 101.

the mule, is from beginning to end a rude negation of their individuality and intelligence; they are habitually addressed and treated as stupid instruments of man's will and pleasure, instead of the highly-organized and sensitive beings that they are. Well might Thoreau, the humanest and most observant of naturalists, complain of man's "not educating the horse, not trying to develop his nature, but merely getting work out of him;" for such, it must be acknowledged, is the prevalent method of treatment, in ninety-nine cases out of a hundred, at the present day, even where there is no actual cruelty or ill-usage.[1]

We are often told that there is no other western country where tame animals are so well treated as in England, and it is only necessary to read the records of a century back to see that the inhumanities of the past were far more atrocious than any that are still practised in the present. Let us be thankful

[1] The representative of an English paper lately had a drive with Count Tolstoi. On his remarking that he had no whip, the Count gave him a glance "almost of scorn," and said, "I talk to my horses; I do not beat them." That this story should have gone the round of the press, as a sort of marvellous legend of a second St. Francis, is a striking comment on the existing state of affairs.

for these facts, as showing that the current of English opinion is at least moving in the right direction. But it must yet be said that the sights that everywhere meet the eye of a humane and thoughtful observer, whether in town or country, are a disgrace to our vaunted "civilization," and suggest the thought that, as far as the touch of compassion is concerned, the majority of our fellow citizens must be obtuse, not to say pachydermatous. Watch the cab traffic in one of the crowded thoroughfares of one of our great cities—always the same lugubrious patient procession of underfed overloaded animals, the same brutal insolence of the drivers, the same accursed sound of the whip. And remembering that these horses are gifted with a large degree of sensibility and intelligence, must one not feel that the fate to which they are thus mercilessly subjected is a shameful violation of the principle which moralists have laid down?

Yet it is to this fate that even the well-kept horses of the rich must in time descend, so to pass the declining years of a life devoted to man's service! "A good man," said Plutarch, "will take care of his horses and dogs, not only while they are young, but when old and past service. We ought certainly not to treat living beings like shoes and household goods, which, when worn out with use, we throw away." Such was the feeling of the old pagan writer, and our good Christians of the present age scarcely seem to have improved on it. True, they do not "throw away" their superannuated carriage-horses—it is so much more lucrative to *sell* them to the shopman or cab-proprietor, who will in due course pass them on to the knacker and cat's-meat man.

The use of machinery is often condemned, on æsthetic grounds, because of the ugliness it has introduced into so many features of modern life. On the other hand, it should not be forgotten that it has immensely relieved the huge mass of animal labour, and that when electricity is generally used for purposes of traction, one of the foulest blots on our social humanity is likely to disappear. Scientific and mechanical invention, so far from being necessarily antagonistic to a true beauty of life, may be found to be of the utmost service to it, when they are employed for humane, and not merely commercial, purposes. Herein Thoreau is a wiser teacher than Ruskin. "If all were as it seems," he says,[1] "and men made the elements their servants for noble

[1] "Walden."

The Case of Domestic Animals

ends! If the cloud that hangs over the engine were the perspiration of heroic deeds, or as beneficent as that which floats over the farmer's fields, then the elements and Nature herself would cheerfully accompany men on their errands and be their escort."

It is no part of my purpose to enumerate the various acts of injustice of which domestic animals are the victims; it is sufficient to point out that the true cause of such injustice is to be sought in the unwarrantable neglect of their many intelligent qualities, and in the contemptuous indifference which, in defiance of sense and reason, still classes them as "brute-beasts." What has been said of horses in this respect applies still more strongly to the second class of domestic animals. Sheep, goats, and oxen are regarded as mere "live-stock;" while pigs, poultry, rabbits, and other marketable "farm-produce," meet with even less consideration, and are constantly treated with very brutal inhumanity by their human possessors.[1] Let anyone who doubts this pay a visit to a cattle-market, and study the scenes that are enacted there.

[1] Further remarks on this subject belong more properly to the Food Question, which is treated in Chapter IV.

The question of the castration of animals may here be briefly referred to. That nothing but imperative necessity could justify such a practice must I think be admitted; for an unnatural mutilation of this kind is not only painful in itself, but deprives those who undergo it of the most vigorous and spirited elements of their character. It is said—with what precise amount of truth I cannot pretend to determine—that man would not otherwise be able to maintain his dominion over the domestic animals; but on the other hand it may be pointed out that this dominion is in no case destined to be perpetuated in its present sharply-accentuated form, and that various practices which, in a sense, are "necessary" now,—*i.e.* in the false position and relationship in which we stand towards the animals,—will doubtless be gradually discontinued under the humaner system of the future. Moreover, castration as performed on cattle, sheep, pigs, and fowls, with no better object than to increase their size and improve their flavour for the table, is, even at the present time, utterly needless and unjustifiable. "The bull," as Shelley says, "must be degraded into the ox, and the ram into the wether, by an unnatural and inhuman operation, that the flaccid fibre

The Case of Domestic Animals 41

may offer a fainter resistance to rebellious nature." In all its aspects, this is a disagreeable subject, and one about which the majority of people do not care to think—probably from an unconscious perception that the established custom could scarcely survive the critical ordeal of thought.

There remains one other class of domestic animals, viz., those who have become still more closely associated with mankind through being the inmates of their homes. The dog is probably better treated on the whole than any other animal;[1] though to prove how far we still are from a rational and consistent appreciation of his worth, it is only necessary to point to the fact that he is commonly regarded by a large number of educated people as a fit and proper subject for that experimental torture which is known as vivisection. The cat has always been treated with far less consideration than the dog, and, despite the numerous scattered instances that might be cited to the contrary, it is to be feared that De Quincey was in the main correct, when he remarked that "the groans and screams of

[1] The use of dogs for purposes of draught was prohibited in London in 1839, and in 1854 this enactment was extended to the whole kingdom.

this poor persecuted race, if gathered into some great echoing hall of horrors, would melt the heart of the stoniest of our race." The institution of "Homes" for lost and starving dogs and cats is a welcome sign of the humane feeling that is asserting itself in some quarters; but it is also no less a proof of the general indifferentism which can allow the most familiar domestic animals to become homeless.

It may be doubted, indeed, whether the condition of the household "pet" is, in the long run, more enviable than that of the "beast of burden." Pets, like kings' favourites, are usually the recipients of an abundance of sentimental affection but of little real kindness; so much easier is it to give temporary caresses than substantial justice. It seems to be forgotten, in a vast majority of cases, that a domestic animal does not exist for the mere idle amusement, any more than for the mere commercial profit, of its human owner; and that for a living being to be turned into a useless puppet is only one degree better than to be doomed to the servitude of a drudge. The injustice done to the pampered lap-dog is as conspicuous, in its way, as that done to the over-worked horse, and both spring from one and the same origin—the fixed belief that the life of a "brute" has no "moral purpose," no distinctive personality worthy of due consideration and development. In a society where the lower animals were regarded as intelligent beings, and not as animated machines, it would be impossible for this incongruous absurdity to continue.

This, then, appears to be our position as regards the rights of domestic animals. Waiving, on the one hand, the somewhat abstruse question whether man is morally justified in utilizing animal labour at all, and on the other the fatuous assertion that he is constituting himself a benefactor by so doing, we recognize that the services of domestic animals have, by immemorial usage, become an important and, it may even be said, necessary element in the economy of modern life. It is impossible, unless every principle of justice is to be cast to the winds, that the due requital of these services should remain a matter of personal caprice; for slavery is at all times hateful and iniquitous, whether it be imposed on mankind or on the lower races. Apart from the universal rights they possess in common with all intelligent beings, domestic animals have a special claim on man's courtesy and sense of fairness, inasmuch as they are not his fellow-creatures only, but his fellow-workers, his dependents, and in many cases the familiar associates and trusted inmates of his home.

CHAPTER III

THE CASE OF WILD ANIMALS

THAT wild animals, no less than domestic animals, have their rights, albeit of a less positive character and far less easy to define, is an essential point which follows directly from the acceptance of the general principle of a *jus animalium*. It is of the utmost importance to emphasize the fact that, whatever the *legal* fiction may have been, or may still be, the rights of animals are not *morally* dependent on the so-called rights of property; it is not to owned animals merely that we must extend our sympathy and protection.

The domination of property has left its trail indelibly on the records of this question. Until the passing of "Martin's Act" in 1822, the most atrocious cruelty, even to domestic animals, could only be punished where there was proved to be an infringement of the rights of ownership.¹ This monstrous iniquity, so far as relates to the domestic animals, has now been removed ; but the only direct legal protection yet accorded to wild animals (except in the Wild Birds' Protection Act of 1880) is that which prohibits their being baited or pitted in conflict ; otherwise, it is open for anyone to kill or torture them with impunity, except where the sacred privileges of "property" are thereby offended. "Everywhere," it has been well said, "it is absolutely a capital crime to be an unowned creature."

Yet surely an unowned creature has the same right as another to live his life unmolested and uninjured except when this is in some way inimical to human welfare. We are justified by the strongest of all instincts, that of self-defence, in safe-guarding ourselves against such a multiplication of any species of animal as might imperil the established supremacy of man ; but we are *not* justified in unnecessarily killing—still less in torturing—any harmless beings whatsoever. In this respect the position of wild animals, in their relation to man, is somewhat analogous to that of the uncivilized towards the civilized nations. No-

[1] See the excellent remarks on this subject in Mr. E. B. Nicholson's "The Rights of an Animal" (ch. III.).

The Case of Wild Animals

thing is more difficult than to determine precisely to what extent it is morally permissible to interfere with the autonomy of savage tribes —an interference which seems in some cases to conduce to the general progress of the race, in others to foster the worst forms of cruelty and injustice; but it is beyond question that savages, like other people, have the right to be exempt from all wanton insult and degradation.

In the same way, while admitting that man is justified, by the exigencies of his own destiny, in asserting his supremacy over the wild animals, we must deny him any right to turn his protectorate into a tyranny, or to inflict one atom more of subjection and pain than is absolutely unavoidable. To take advantage of the sufferings of animals, whether wild or tame, for the gratification of sport, or gluttony, or fashion, is quite incompatible with any possible assertion of animals' rights. We may kill, if necessary, but never torture or degrade.

"The laws of self-defence," says an old writer,[1] "undoubtedly justify us in destroying those animals who would destroy us, who in-

[1] "On Cruelty to the Inferior Animals," by Soame Jenyns, 1782.

jure our properties or annoy our persons ; but not even these, whenever their situation incapacitates them from hurting us. I know of no right which we have to shoot a bear on an inaccessible island of ice, or an eagle on the mountain's top, whose lives cannot injure us, nor deaths procure us any benefit. We are unable to give life, and therefore ought not to take it away from the meanest insect without sufficient reason."

I reserve, for fuller consideration in subsequent chapters, certain problems which are suggested by the wholesale slaughter of wild animals by the huntsman or the trapper, for purposes which are loosely supposed to be necessary and inevitable. Meantime a word must be said about the condition of those tamed or caged animals which, though wild by nature, and not bred in captivity, are yet to a certain extent "domesticated"—a class which stands midway between the true domestic and the wild. Is the imprisonment of such animals a violation of the principle we have laid down? In most cases I fear this question can only be answered in the affirmative.

And here, once more I must protest against the common assumption that these captive

The Case of Wild Animals

animals are laid *under an obligation* to man by the very fact of their captivity, and that therefore no complaint can be made on the score of their loss of freedom and the many miseries involved therein! It is extraordinary that even humane thinkers and earnest champions of animals' rights, should permit themselves to be misled by this most fallacious and flimsy line of argument. "Harmful animals," says one of these writers,[1] "and animals with whom man has to struggle for the fruits of the earth, may of course be so shut up: they gain by it, for otherwise they would not have been let live."

And so in like manner it is sometimes contended that a menagerie is a sort of paradise for wild beasts, whose loss of liberty is more than compensated by the absence of the constant apprehension and insecurity which, it is conveniently assumed, weigh so heavily on their spirits. But all this notion of their "gaining by it" is in truth nothing more than a mere arbitrary supposition; for, in the first place, a speedy death may, for all we know, be very preferable to a protracted death-in-life; while, secondly, the pretence that wild animals enjoy captivity is even more absurd than the episcopal contention[2] that the life of

[1] Mr. E. B. Nicholson. [2] See p. 32.

a domestic animal is "one of very great comfort, according to the animal's own standard."

To take a wild animal from its free natural state, full of abounding egoism and vitality, and to shut it up for the wretched remainder of its life in a cell where it has just space to turn round, and where it necessarily loses every distinctive feature of its character—this appears to me to be as downright a denial as could well be imagined of the theory of animals' rights.[1] Nor is there very much force in the plea founded on the alleged scientific value of these zoological institutions, at any rate in the case of the wilder and less tractable animals, for it cannot be maintained that the establishment of wild-beast shows is in any way necessary for the advancement of human knowledge. For what do the good people see

---

[1] I subjoin a sentence, copied by me from one of the note-books of the late James Thomson ("B.V."): "It being a very wet Sunday, I had to keep in, and paced much prisoner-like to and fro my room. This reminded me of the wild beasts at Regent's Park, and especially of the great wild birds, the vultures and eagles. How they must suffer! How long will it be ere the thought of such agonies becomes intolerable to the public conscience, and wild creatures be left at liberty when they need not be killed? Three or four centuries, perhaps."

The Case of Wild Animals 51

who go to the gardens on a half-holiday afternoon to poke their umbrellas at a blinking eagle-owl, or to throw dog-biscuits down the expansive throat of a hippopotamus? Not wild beasts or wild birds certainly, for there never have been or can be such in the best of all possible menageries, but merely the outer semblances and *simulacra* of the denizens of forest and prairie—poor spiritless remnants of what were formerly wild animals. To kill and stuff these victims of our morbid curiosity, instead of immuring them in lifelong imprisonment, would be at once a humaner and a cheaper method, and could not possibly be of less use to science.[1]

But of course these remarks do not apply, with anything like the same force, to the taming of such wild animals as are readily domesticated in captivity, or trained by man to some intelligible and practical purpose. For example, though we may look forward to

[1] Unfortunately they are not of much value even for *that* purpose, owing to the deterioration of health and vigour caused by their imprisonment. "The skeletons of aged carnivora," says Dr. W. B. Carpenter, "are often good for nothing as museum specimens, their bones being rickety and distorted." Could there be a more convincing proof than this of the inhumanity of these exhibitions?

the time when it will not be deemed necessary to convert wild elephants into beasts of burden, it must be acknowledged that the exaction of such service, however questionable in itself, is very different from condemning an animal to a long term of useless and deadening imbecility. There can be no absolute standard of morals in these matters, whether it be human liberty or animal liberty that is at stake; I merely contend that it is as incumbent on us to show good reason for curtailing the one as the other. This would be at once recognised, but for the prevalent habit of regarding the lower animals as devoid of moral purpose and individuality.

The caging of wild song-birds is another practice which deserves the strongest reprobation. It is often pleaded that the amusement given by these unfortunate prisoners to the still more unfortunate human prisoners of the sick-room, or the smoky city, is a justification for their sacrifice; but surely such excuses rest only on habit—habitual inability or unwillingness to look facts in the face. Few invalids, I fancy, would be greatly cheered by the captive life that hangs at their window, if they had fully considered how blighted and sterilized a life it must be. The bird-catcher's trade and

The Case of Wild Animals

the bird-catcher's shop are alike full of horrors, and they are horrors which are due entirely to a silly fashion and a habit of callous thoughtlessness, not on the part of the ruffianly bird-catcher (ruffianly enough, too often,) who has to bear the burden of the odium attaching to these cruelties, but of the respectable customers who buy captured larks and linnets without the smallest scruple or consideration.

Finally, let me point out that if we desire to cultivate a closer intimacy with the wild animals, it must be an intimacy based on a genuine love for them as living beings and fellow-creatures, not on the superior power or cunning by which we can drag them from their native haunts, warp the whole purpose of their lives, and degrade them to the level of pets, or curiosities, or labour-saving automata. The key to a proper understanding of the wild, as of the tame, animals must always lie in such sympathies—sympathies, as Wordsworth describes them,

> "Aloft ascending, and descending deep,
> Even to the inferior Kinds ; whom forest trees
> Protect from beating sunbeams and the sweep
> Of the sharp winds ; fair Creatures, to whom Heaven
> A calm and sinless life, with love, has given."

CHAPTER IV

THE SLAUGHTER OF ANIMALS FOR FOOD

IT is impossible that any discussion of the principle of animals' rights can be at all adequate or conclusive which ignores, as many so-called humanitarians still ignore, the immense underlying importance of the food question. The origin of the habit of flesh-eating need not greatly concern us; let us assume, in accordance with the most favoured theory, that animals were first slaughtered by the uncivilized migratory tribes under the stress of want, and that the practice thus engendered, being fostered by the religious idea of blood-offering and propitiation, survived and increased after the early conditions which produced it had passed away. What is more important to note, is that the very prevalence of the habit has caused it to be regarded as a necessary feature of modern civilisation, and that this view has inevitably had a marked

The Slaughter of Animals for Food

effect, and a very detrimental effect, on the study of man's moral relation to the lower animals.

Now it must be admitted, I think, that it is a difficult thing consistently to recognise or assert the rights of an animal on whom you purpose to make a meal, a difficulty which has not been at all satisfactorily surmounted by those moralists who, while accepting the practice of flesh-eating as an institution which is itself beyond cavil, have nevertheless been anxious to find some solid basis for a theory of humaneness. "Strange contrariety of conduct," says Goldsmith's "Chinese Philosopher," in commenting on this dilemma; "they pity, and they *eat* the objects of their compassion!" There is also the further consideration that the sanction implicitly given to the terrible cruelties inflicted on harmless cattle by the drover and the slaughterman render it, by parity of reasoning, well-nigh impossible to abolish many other acts of injustice that we see everywhere around us; and this obstacle the opponents of humanitarian reform have not been slow to utilise.[1] Hence a disposition

---

[1] Here are two instances urged on behalf of the vivisector and the sportsman respectively. "If man can legitimately put animals to a painful death in

on the part of many otherwise humane writers to fight shy of the awkward subject of the slaughterhouse, or to gloss it over with a series of contradictory and quite irrelevant excuses.

Let me give a few examples. "We deprive animals of life," says Bentham, in a delightfully naïve application of the utilitarian philosophy, "and this is justifiable; their pains do not equal our enjoyments."

"By the scheme of universal providence," says Lawrence, "the services between man and beast are intended to be reciprocal, and the greater part of the latter can by no other means requite human labour and care than by the forfeiture of life."

Schopenhauer's plea is somewhat similar to the foregoing: "Man deprived of all flesh food, especially in the north, would suffer more than the animal suffers in a swift and unfore-

---

order to supply himself with food and luxuries, why may he not also legitimately put them to pain, and even to death, for the higher object of relieving the sufferings of humanity?"—*Chambers's Encyclopædia*, 1884.

"If they were called upon to put an end to pigeon-shooting, they might next be called upon to put an end to the slaughter of live-stock."—LORD FORTESCUE, *Debate on Pigeon-Shooting* (1884).

The Slaughter of Animals for Food

seen death ; still we ought to mitigate it by the help of chloroform."

Then there is the argument so frequently founded on the supposed sanction of Nature. " My scruples," wrote Lord Chesterfield, " remained unreconciled to the committing of so horrid a meal, till upon serious reflection I became convinced of its legality from the general order of Nature, which has instituted the universal preying upon the weaker as one of her first principles."

Finally, we find the redoubtable Paley discarding as valueless the whole appeal to Nature, and relying on the ordinances of Holy Writ. " A right to the flesh of animals. Some excuse seems necessary for the pain and loss which we occasion to animals by restraining them of their liberty, mutilating their bodies, and at last putting an end to their lives for our pleasure or convenience. The reasons alleged in vindication of this practice are the following : that the several species of animals being created to prey upon one another affords a kind of analogy to prove that the human species were intended to feed upon them. . . . Upon which reason I would observe that the analogy contended for is extremely lame, since animals have no power to support life by any other means, and since we have, for the whole human species might subsist entirely upon fruit, pulse, herbs, and roots, as many tribes of Hindus actually do. . . . It seems to me that it would be difficult to defend this right by any arguments which the light and order of Nature afford, and that we are beholden for it to the permission recorded in Scripture."

It is evident from the above quotations, which might be indefinitely extended, that the fable of the Wolf and the Lamb is constantly repeating itself in the attitude of our moralists and philosophers towards the victims of the slaughter-house! Well might Humphry Primatt remark that "we ransack and rack all nature in her weakest and tenderest parts, to extort from her, if possible, any concession whereon to rest the appearance of an argument."

Far wiser and humaner, on this particular subject, is the tone adopted by such writers as Michelet, who, while not seeing any way of escape from the practice of flesh-eating, at least refrain from attempting to support it by fallacious reasonings. "The animals below us," says Michelet, "have also their rights before God. Animal life, sombre mystery!

The Slaughter of Animals for Food

Immense world of thoughts and of dumb sufferings! All nature protests against the barbarity of man, who misapprehends, who humiliates, who tortures his inferior brethren. . . . . Life—death! The daily murder which feeding upon animals implies—those hard and bitter problems sternly placed themselves before my mind. Miserable contradiction! Let us hope that there may be another globe in which the base, the cruel fatalities of this may be spared to us."[1]

Meantime, however, the simple fact remains true, and is every year finding more and more scientific corroboration, that there is no such "cruel fatality" as that which Michelet imagined. Comparative anatomy has shown that man is not carnivorous, but frugivorous, in his natural structure; experience has shown that flesh-food is wholly unnecessary for the support of healthy life. The importance of this more general recognition of a truth which has in all ages been familiar to a few enlightened thinkers, can hardly be over-estimated in its bearing on the question of animals' rights. It clears away a difficulty which has long damped the enthusiasm, or warped the judgment, of the humaner school of European moralists,

[1] "La Bible de l'Humanité."

and makes it possible to approach the subject of man's moral relation to the lower animals in a more candid and fearless spirit of enquiry. It is no part of my present purpose to advocate the cause of vegetarianism; but in view of the mass of evidence, readily obtainable,[1] that the transit and slaughter of animals are necessarily attended by most atrocious cruelties, and that a large number of persons have for years been living healthily without the use of flesh-meat, it must at least be said that to omit this branch of the subject from the most earnest and strenuous consideration is playing with the question of animals' rights. Fifty or a hundred years ago, there was perhaps some excuse for supposing that vegetarianism was a mere fad; there is absolutely no such excuse at the present time.

There are two points of especial significance in this connection. First, that as civilisation advances, the cruelties inseparable from the slaughtering system have been aggravated rather than diminished, owing both to the

[1] From any of the following societies: The Vegetarian Society, 75, Princess Street, Manchester; the London Vegetarian Society, Memorial Hall, E.C.; the National Food Reform Society, 13, Rathbone Place, W.

The Slaughter of Animals for Food 61

increased necessity of transporting animals long distances by sea and land, under conditions of hurry and hardship which generally preclude any sort of humane regard for their comfort, and to the clumsy and barbarous methods of slaughtering too often practised in those ill-constructed dens of torment known as "private slaughter-houses."[1]

Secondly, that the feeling of repugnance caused among all people of sensibility and refinement by the sight, or mention, or even thought, of the business of the butcher are also largely on the increase; so that the details of the revolting process are, as far as possible, kept carefully out of sight and out of mind, being delegated to a pariah class who do the work which most educated persons would shrink from doing for themselves. In these two facts we have clear evidence, first that there is good reason why the public conscience, or at any rate the humanitarian conscience, should be uneasy concerning the slaughter of "live-stock," and secondly that this uneasiness

---

[1] If any reader thinks there is exaggeration in this statement, let him study (1) "Cattle Ships," by Samuel Plimsoll, Kegan Paul, Trench, Trubner and Co., 1890; (2) "Behind the Scenes in Slaughter-houses," by H. F. Lester, Wm. Reeves, 1892.

is already to a large extent developed and manifested.

The common argument, adopted by many apologists of flesh-eating, as of fox-hunting, that the pain inflicted by the death of the animals is more than compensated by the pleasure enjoyed by them in their life-time, since otherwise they would not have been brought into existence at all, is ingenious rather than convincing, being indeed none other than the old familiar fallacy already commented on—the arbitrary trick of constituting ourselves the spokesmen and the interpreters of our victims. Mr. E. B. Nicholson, for example, is of opinion that "we may pretty safely take it that if he [the fox] were able to understand and answer the question, he would choose life, with all its pains and risks, to non-existence without them."[1] Unfortunately for the soundness of this suspiciously partial assumption, there is no recorded instance of this strange alternative having ever been submitted either to fox or philosopher; so that a precedent has yet to be established on which to found a judgment. Meantime, instead of committing the gross absurdity of talking of non-existence as a state

[1] "The Rights of an Animal," 1879.

which is good, or bad, or in any way comparable to existence, we might do well to remember that animals' rights, if we admit them at all, must begin with the birth, and can only end with the death, of the animals in question, and that we cannot evade our just responsibilities by any such quibbling references to an imaginary ante-natal choice in an imaginary ante-natal condition.

The most mischievous effect of the practice of flesh-eating, in its influence on the study of animals' rights at the present time, is that it so stultifies and debases the very *raison d'être* of countless myriads of beings—it brings them into life for no better purpose than to deny their right to live. It is idle to appeal to the internecine warfare that we see in some aspects of wild nature, where the weaker animal is often the prey of the stronger, for there (apart from the fact that co-operation largely modifies competition) the weaker races at least live their own lives and take their chance in the game, whereas the victims of the human carnivora are bred, and fed, and from the first predestined to untimely slaughter, so that their whole mode of living is warped from its natural standard, and they are scarcely more than animated beef or mutton or pork. This, I contend, is a flagrant violation of the rights of the lower animals, as those rights are now beginning to be apprehended by the humaner conscience of mankind. It has been well said that "to keep a man (slave or servant) for your own advantage merely, to keep an animal that you may *eat* it, is a lie. You cannot look that man or animal in the face."[1]

That those who are aware of the horrors involved in slaughtering, and also aware of the possibility of a fleshless diet, should think it sufficient to oppose "scriptural permission" as an answer to the arguments of food-reformers is an instance of the extraordinary power of custom to blind the eyes and the hearts of otherwise humane men. The following passage is quoted from a "Plea for Mercy to Animals,"[2] as a typical instance of the sort of perverted sentiment to which I allude. "Not in superstitious India only," says the writer, whose ideas of what constitutes "superstition" seem to be rather confused, "but in this country, there are vegetarians, and other persons, who object to the use of animal food, not on the ground of health only, but as involving

[1] Edward Carpenter, "England's Ideal."
[2] By J. Macaulay (Partridge and Co., 1881).

a power to which man has no right. To such statements we have only to oppose the clear permission of the divine Author of life. But the unqualified permission can never give sanction to the infliction of unnecessary pain."

But if the use of flesh-meat can itself be dispensed with, how can it be argued that the pain, which is inseparable from slaughtering, can be otherwise than unnecessary also? I trust that the cause of humanity and justice (not "mercy") to the lower animals is not likely to be retarded by any such sentimental and superstitious objections as these!

Reform of diet will doubtless be slow, and attended in many individual cases with its difficulties and drawbacks. But at least we may lay down this much as incumbent on all humanitarian thinkers—that everyone must satisfy himself of the necessity, the real necessity, of the use of flesh-food, before he comes to any intellectual conclusion on the subject of animals' rights. It is easy to see that, as the question is more and more discussed, the result will be more and more decisive. "Whatever my own practice may be," wrote Thoreau, "I have no doubt that it is a part of the destiny of the human race, in its gradual improvement, to leave off eating animals, as surely as the savage tribes have left off eating each other when they came in contact with the more civilized."

CHAPTER V

SPORT, OR AMATEUR BUTCHERY

THAT particular form of recreation which is euphemistically known as "sport" has a close historical connection with the practice of flesh-eating, inasmuch as the hunter was in old times what the butcher is now,—the "purveyor" on whom the family was dependent for its daily supply of victuals. Modern sport, however, as usually carried on in civilised European countries, has degenerated into what has been well described as "amateur butchery," a system under which the slaughter of certain kinds of animals is practised less as a necessity than as a means of amusement and diversion. Just as the youthful nobles, during the savage scenes and reprisals of the Huguenot wars, used to seize the opportunity of exercising their swordsmanship, and perfecting themselves in the art of dealing graceful death-blows, so the modern sportsman converts the killing of animals from a prosaic and perhaps distasteful business into an agreeable and gentlemanly pastime.

Now, on the very face of it, this amateur butchery is, in one sense, the most wanton and indefensible of all possible violations of the principle of animals' rights. If animals—or men, for that matter—have of necessity to be killed, let them be killed accordingly; but to seek one's own amusement out of the death-pangs of other beings, this is saddening stupidity indeed! Wisely did Wordsworth inculcate as the moral of his " Hartleap Well,"

> " Never to blend our pleasure or our pride
> With sorrow of the meanest thing that feels."

But the sporting instinct is due to sheer callousness and insensibility; the sportsman, by force of habit, or by force of hereditary influence, cannot understand or sympathize with the sufferings he causes, and being, in the great majority of instances, a man of slow perception, he naturally finds it much easier to follow the hounds than to follow an argument. And here, in his chief blame, lies also his chief excuse; for it may be said of him, as it cannot be said of certain other tormentors, that he really does not comprehend the import of what

Sport, or Amateur Butchery 69

he is doing. Whether this ultimately makes his position better or worse, is a point for the casuist to decide.

That "it would have to be killed anyhow" is a truly deplorable reason for torturing any animal whatsoever; it is an argument which would equally have justified the worst barbarities of the Roman amphitheatre. To exterminate wolves, and other dangerous species, may indeed, at certain places and times, be necessary and justifiable enough. But the sportsman nowadays will not even perform this practical service of exterminating such animals—the fox, for example—as are noxious to the general interests of the community; on the contrary, he "preserves" them (note the unintended humour of the term!), and then, by a happy afterthought, claims the gratitude of the animals themselves for his humane and benevolent interposition.[1] In plain words, he first undertakes to rid the country of a pest, and then, finding the process an enjoyable one to himself, he contrives that it shall never be

---

[1] I copy the following typical argument from a recent article in a London paper. "If we stay fox-hunting—which sport makes something of some of us—foxes will die far more brutal deaths in cruel vermin-traps, until there are none left to die."

brought to a conclusion. Prometheus had precisely as much reason to be grateful to the vulture for eternally gnawing at his liver, as have the hunted animals to thank the predaceous sportsmen who "preserve" them. Let me once more enter a protest against the canting Pharisaism which is afraid to take the just responsibility of its own selfish pleasure-seeking.

"What name should we bestow," said a humane essayist of the eighteenth century,[1] "on a superior being who, without provocation or advantage, should continue from day to day, void of all pity and remorse, to torment mankind for diversion, and at the same time endeavour with the utmost care to preserve their lives and to propagate their species, in order to increase the number of victims devoted to his malevolence, and be delighted in proportion to the miseries which he occasioned? I say, what name detestable enough could we find for such a being? Yet, if we impartially consider the case, and our intermediate situation, we must acknowledge that, with regard to the inferior animals, just such a being is the sportsman."

The excuses alleged in favour of English

[1] Soame Jenyns, 1782.

Sport, or Amateur Butchery

field-sports in general, and of hunting in particular, are for the most part as irrelevant as they are unreasonable. It is often said that the manliness of our national character would be injuriously affected by the discontinuance of these sports—a strange argument, when one considers the very unequal, and therefore unmanly, conditions of the strife. But, apart from this consideration, what right can we possess to cultivate these personal qualities at the expense of unspeakable suffering to the lower races? Such actions may be pardonable in a savage, or in a schoolboy in whom the savage nature still largely predominates, but they are wholly unworthy of a civilised and rational man.

As for the nonsense sometimes talked about the beneficial effects of those field-sports which bring men into contact with the sublimities of nature, I will only repeat what I have elsewhere said on this subject, that "the dynamiters who cross the ocean to blow up an English town might on this principle justify the object of their journey by the assertion that the sea-voyage brought them in contact with the exalting and ennobling influence of the Atlantic."[1]

[1] As further example of the stuff to which the apolo-

As the case stands between the sportsman and his victims, there cannot be much doubt as to whence the benefits proceed, and from which party the gratitude is due. "Woe to the ungrateful!" says Michelet. "By this phrase I mean the sporting crowd, who, unmindful of the numerous benefits we owe to the animals, exterminate innocent life. A terrible sentence weighs on the tribes of sportsmen—they can create nothing. They originate no art, no industry.... It is a shocking and hideous thing to see a child partial to sport; to see woman enjoying and admiring murder, and encouraging her child. That delicate and sensitive woman would not give him a knife, but she gives him a gun."

The sports of hunting and coursing are a brutality which could not be tolerated for a day in a state which possessed anything more than the mere name of justice, freedom, and enlightenment. " Nor can they comprehend," says Sir Thomas More of his model citizens

gists of sport are reduced in their search for an argument, the following may be cited. " For what object was given the scent of the hound, and the exultation with which he abandons himself to the chase? If he were not thus employed, for what valuable purpose could he be used?"

Sport, or Amateur Butchery

in "Utopia," "the pleasure of seeing dogs run after a hare more than of seeing one dog run after another; for if the seeing them run is that which gives the pleasure, you have the same entertainment to the eye on both these occasions, since that is the same in both cases; but if the pleasure lies in seeing the hare killed and torn by the dogs, this ought rather to stir pity, that a weak, harmless, and fearful hare should be devoured by strong, fierce, and cruel dogs."

To be accurate, the zest of sport lies neither in the running nor the killing, as such, but in the excitement caused by the fact that a life (some one else's life) is at stake, that the pursuer is matched in a fierce game of hazard against the pursued. The opinion has been expressed, by one well qualified to speak with authority on the subject, that "well-laid drags, tracked by experts, would test the mettle both of hounds and riders to hounds, but then a terrified, palpitating, fleeing life would not be struggling ahead, and so the idea is not pleasing to those who find pleasure in blood.[1]

The case is even worse when the quarry is to all intents and purposes domesticated, an

[1] "The Horrors of Sport," by Lady Florence Dixie, 1892.

animal wild by nature, but by force of circumstances and surroundings tame. Such are the Ascot stags, the victims of the Royal Sport, which is one of the last and least justifiable relics of feudal barbarism.[1] I would here remark that there is urgent need that the laws which relate to the humane treatment of animals should be amended, or more wisely interpreted, on this particular point, so as to afford immediate protection to these domesticated stags, whose torture, under the name and sanction of the Crown and the State, has been long condemned by the public conscience. Bear-baiting and cock-fighting have now been abolished by legal enactment, and it is high time that the equally demoralising sport of hunting of tame stags should be relegated to the same category.[2]

[1] See "Royal Sport, some Facts concerning the Queen's Buckhounds," by the Rev. J. Stratton.

[2] As long ago as 1877 a prosecution for the torture of a hind by the Royal Buckhounds was instituted by the Society for the Prevention of Cruelty to Animals. The hind was worried for more than an hour by six hounds, and fearfully mutilated. But though a dozen eye-witnesses were forthcoming, and the skin of the animal was in possession of the Society (it may be seen to this day at the office in Jermyn Street), the case was dismissed by the magistrates on the absurd

Sport, or Amateur Butchery

The same must be said of some sports which are practised by the English working man—rabbit-coursing, in particular, that half-holiday diversion which is so popular in many villages of the North.[1] An attempt is often made by the apologists of amateur butchery to play off one class against another in the discussion of this question. They protest, on the one hand, against any interference with aristocratic sport, on the plea that working men are no less addicted to such pastimes; and, on the other hand, a cry is raised against the unfairness of restricting the amusements of the poor, while noble lords and ladies are permitted to hunt the carted stag with impunity.

The obvious answer to these quibbling excuses is that *all* such barbarities, whether practised by rich or poor, are alike condemned by any conceivable principle of justice and humaneness; and, further, that it is a doubtful compliment to working men to suggest that they have nothing better to do in their spare hours than to torture defenceless rabbits. It

---

ground that a stag is *feræ naturæ*, and all evidence and argument were thus purposely shut out. See the "Animal World" for June 1st, 1877.

[1] See "Rabbit-Coursing, an Appeal to Working Men," by Dr. R. H. Jude, 1892.

was long ago remarked by Martin, the author of the famous Act of 1822, that such an argument indicates at bottom a contempt rather than regard for the working classes; it is as much as to say, "Poor creatures, let them alone—they have few amusements—let them enjoy them."

Nothing can be more shocking than the treatment commonly accorded to rabbits, rats, and other small animals, on the plea that they are "vermin," and therefore, it is tacitly assumed, outside the pale of humanity and justice; we have here another instance of the way in which the application of a contemptuous name may aggravate and increase the actual tendency to barbarous ill-usage How many a demoralising spectacle, especially where the young are concerned, is witnessed when "fun" is made out of the death and torture of "vermin!" How horrible is the practice, apparently universal throughout all country districts, of setting steel traps along the ditches and hedgerows, in which the victims are frequently left to linger, in an agony of pain and apprehension, for hours or even days! If the lower races have any rights soever, here surely is a flagrant and inexcusable outrage on such rights. Yet there are

Sport, or Amateur Butchery 77

no means of redressing these barbarities, because the laws, such as they are, which prohibit cruelty to animals, are not designed to take any cognizance of " vermin."

All that has been said of hunting and coursing is applicable also—in a less degree, perhaps, but on exactly the same principle—to the sports of shooting and fishing. It does not in the least matter, so far as the question of animals' rights is concerned, whether you run your victim to death with a pack of yelping hounds, or shoot him with a gun, or drag him from his native waters by a hook; the point at issue is simply whether man is justified in inflicting any form of death or suffering on the lower races for his mere amusement and caprice. There can be little doubt what answer must be given to this question.

In concluding this chapter, let me quote a striking testimony to the wickedness and injustice of sport, as exhibited in one of its most refined and fashionable forms, the " cult of the pheasant." " For what is it," says Lady Florence Dixie,[1] " but the deliberate massacre in cold blood every year of thousands and tens of thousands of tame, hand-reared birds who are literally driven into the jaws of death

[1] Letter to " Pall Mall Gazette," March 24th, 1892.

and mown down in a peculiarly brutal manner? . . . A perfect roar of guns fills the air, louder tap and yell the beaters, above the din can be heard the heart-rending cries of wounded hares and rabbits, some of which can be seen dragging themselves away, with both hind legs broken, or turning round and round in their agony before they die. And the pheasants! They are on every side, some rising, some dropping, some lying dead, but the greater majority fluttering on the ground wounded, some with both legs broken and a wing, some with both wings broken and a leg, others merely winged, running to hide, others mortally wounded gasping out their last breath of life amidst the fiendish sounds which surround them. And this is called *sport!* . . . Sport in every form and kind is horrible, from the rich man's hare-coursing to the poor man's rabbit-coursing. All show the 'tiger' that lives in our natures, and which nothing but a higher civilisation will eradicate."

CHAPTER VI

MURDEROUS MILLINERY

WE have seen what a vast amount of quite preventable suffering is caused through the agency of the slaughterman, who kills for a business, and of the sportsman who kills for a pastime, the victims in either case being regarded as mere irrational automata, with no higher destiny than to satisfy the most artificial wants or the most cruel caprices of mankind. A few words must now be said about the fur and feather traffic—the slaughter of mammals and birds for human clothing or human ornamentation—a subject connected on the one hand with that of flesh-eating, and on the other, though to a less degree, with that of sport. What I shall say will of course have no reference to wool, or any other substance which is obtainable without injury to the animal from which it is taken.

It is evident that in this case, as in the

butchering trade, the responsibility for whatever wrongs are done must rest ultimately on the class which demands an unnecessary commodity, rather than on that which is compelled by economic pressure to supply it; it is not the man who kills the bird, but the lady who wears the feathers in her hat, who is the true offender. But here it will be asked, *is* the use of fur and feathers unnecessary? Now of course if we consider solely the present needs and tastes of society, in regard to these matters, it must be admitted that a sudden, unexpected withdrawal of the numberless animal products on which our "civilisation" depends would be a very serious embarrassment; the world, as alarmists point out to us, might have to go to bed without candles, and wake up to find itself without boots. It must be remembered, however, that such changes do not come about with suddenness, but, on the contrary, with the extremest slowness imaginable; and a little thought will suggest, what experience has already in many cases confirmed, that there is really no indispensable animal substance for which a substitute cannot be provided, when once there is sufficient demand, from the vegetable or mineral kingdom.

Take the case of leather, for instance, a

Murderous Millinery

material which is in almost universal use, and may, under present circumstances, be fairly described as a necessary. What should we do without leather? was, in fact, a question very frequently asked of vegetarians during the early and callow years of the food-reform movement, until it was found that vegetable leather could be successfully employed in boot-making, and that the inconsistency of which vegetarians at present stand convicted is only a temporary and incidental one. Now of course, so long as oxen are slaughtered for food, their skins will be utilized in this way; but it is not difficult to foresee that the gradual discontinuance of the habit of flesh-eating will lead to a similar gradual discontinuance of the use of hides, and that human ingenuity will not be at a loss in the provision of a substitute. So that it does not follow that a commodity which, in the immediate sense, is necessary now, would be absolutely or permanently necessary, under different conditions, in the future.

My sole reason for dwelling on this typical point is that I wish to guard myself, by anticipation, against a very plausible argument, by which discredit is often cast on the whole theory of animals' rights. What can be the object, it is said, of entering on the sentimental path of an impossible humanitarianism, which only leads into insurmountable difficulties and dilemmas, inasmuch as the use of these various animal substances is so interwoven with the whole system of society that it can never be discontinued until society itself comes to an end? I assert that the case is by no means so desperate—that it is easy to make a right beginning now, and to foresee the lines along which future progress will be effected. Much that is impossible in our own time may be realized, by those who come after us, as the natural and inevitable outcome of reforms which it now lies with us to inaugurate.

This said, it may be freely admitted that, at the outset, humanitarians will do well to draw a practical distinction between such animal products as are converted to some genuine personal use, and those which are supplied for no better object than to gratify the idle whims of luxury or fashion. The *when* and the *where* are considerations of the greatest import in these questions. There is a certain fitness in the hunter—himself the product of a rough, wild era in human development—assuming the skins of the wild creatures he has

Murderous Millinery

conquered; but it does not follow because an Eskimo, for example, may appropriately wear fur, or a Red Indian feathers, that this apparel will be equally becoming to the inhabitants of London or New York; on the contrary, an act which is perfectly natural in the one case, is often a sign of crass vulgarity in the other. Hercules, clothed triumphant in the spoils of the Nemean lion, is a subject for painter and poet; but what if he had purchased the skin, ready dressed, from a contemporary manufacturer?

What we must unhesitatingly condemn is the blind and reckless barbarism which has ransacked, and is ransacking, whole provinces and continents, without a glimmer of suspicion that the innumerable birds and quadrupeds which it is rapidly exterminating have any other part or purpose in nature than to be sacrificed to human vanity, that idle gentlemen and ladies may bedeck themselves, like certain characters in the fable, in borrowed skins and feathers. What care *they* for all the beauty and tenderness and intelligence of the varied forms of animal life? and what is it to them whether these be helped forward by man in the universal progress and evolution of all living things, or whether whole species be transformed and degraded by the way—boiled down, like the beaver, into a hat, or, like the seal, into a lady's jacket?[1]

Whatever it may be in other respects, the fur trade, in so far as it is a supply of ornamental clothing for those who are under no necessity of wearing fur at all, is a barbarous and stupid business. It makes patch-work, one may say, not only of the hides of its victims, but of the conscience and intellect of its supporters. A fur garment or trimming, we are told, appearing to the eye as if it were one uniform piece, is generally made up of many curiously shaped fragments. It is significant that a society which is enamoured of so many shams and fictions, and which detests nothing so strongly as the need of looking facts in the face, should pre-eminently esteem those articles of apparel which are constructed on the most deceptive and illusory principle. The story of the Ass in the Lion's skin is capable, it seems, of a new and wider application.

---

[1] It is stated of the fur-seal of Alaska (*callorhinus ursinus*) that "there is no known animal, on land or water, which can take higher physical rank, or which exhibits a higher order of instinct, closely approaching human intelligence."—*Chambers' Journal*, Nov. 27th, 1886.

Murderous Millinery

But if the fur trade gives cause for serious reflection, what are we to say of the still more abominable trade in feathers? Murderous, indeed, is the millinery which finds its most fashionable ornament in the dead bodies of birds—birds, the loveliest and most blithesome beings in Nature! There is a pregnant remark made by a writer in the "Encyclopædia Britannica," that "to enumerate all the feathers used for ornamental purposes would be practically to give a complete list of all known and obtainable birds." The figures and details published by those humane writers who have raised an unavailing protest against this latest and worst crime of Fashion are simply appalling in their stern and naked record of unremitting cruelty.

"One dealer in London is said to have received as a single consignment 32,000 dead humming-birds, 80,000 aquatic birds, and 800,000 pairs of wings. A Parisian dealer had a contract for 40,000 birds, and an army of murderers were turned out to supply the order. No less than 40,000 terns have been sent from Long Island in one season for millinery purposes. At one auction alone in London there were sold 404,389 West Indian and Brazilian bird-skins, and 356,389 East

Indian, besides thousands of pheasants and birds-of-paradise."[1] The meaning of such statistics is simply that the women of Europe and America have given an order for the ruthless extermination of birds.[2]

It is not seriously contended in any quarter that this wholesale destruction, effected often in the most revolting and heartless manner,[3] is capable of excuse or justification; yet the efforts of those who address themselves to the better feelings of the offenders appear to meet with little or no success. The cause of this failure must undoubtedly be sought in the general lack of any clear conviction that animals have rights; and the evil will never be thoroughly remedied until not only this particular abuse, but all such abuses, and the prime source from which such abuses originate, have been subjected to an impartial criticism.[4]

---

[1] Quoted from "As in a Mirror, an Appeal to the Ladies of England."

[2] "You kill a paddy-bird," says an Indian proverb, "and what do you get? A handful of feathers." Unfortunately commerce has now taught the natives of India that a handful of feathers is not without its value.

[3] See the publications issued by the Society for the Protection of Birds, 29, Warwick Road, Maida Vale, W.

[4] It is well that ladies should pledge themselves to

Murderous Millinery

In saying this I do not of course mean to imply that special efforts should not be directed against special cruelties. I have already remarked that the main responsibility for the daily murders which fashionable millinery is instigating must lie at the doors of those who demand, rather than those who supply, these hideous and funereal ornaments. Unfor-

a rule of not wearing feathers; but that is an ominous exception which permits them to wear the feathers of birds killed for food. It is to such inconsistencies that an anonymous satirist makes reference in the following lines:

"When Edwin sat him down to dine one night,
  With piteous grief his heart was newly stricken;
In vain did Angelina him invite,
  Grace said, to carve the chicken.

"'A thousand songsters slaughtered in one day;
  Oh, Angelina, meditate upon it;
And henceforth never, never wear, I pray,
  A redbreast in thy bonnet.'

"Fair Angelina did not scold nor scowl;
  No word she spake, she better knew her lover;
But from the ample dish of roasted fowl
  She gently raised the cover.

"And lo! the savour of that tender bird
  The tender Edwin's appetite did quicken.
He started, by a new emotion stirred,
  Said grace, and carved the chicken."

tunately the process, like that of slaughtering cattle, is throughout delegated to other hands than those of the ultimate purchaser, so that it is exceedingly difficult to bring home a due sense of blood-guiltiness to the right person.

The confirmed sportsman, or amateur butcher, at least sees with his own eyes the circumstances attendant on his "sport;" and the fact that he feels no compunction in pursuing it, is due, in most cases, to an obtuseness or confusion of the moral faculties. But many of those who wear seal-skin mantles, or feather-bedaubed bonnets are naturally humane enough; they are misled by pure ignorance or thoughtlessness, and would at once abandon such practices if they could be made aware of the methods employed in the wholesale massacre of seals or humming-birds. Still, it remains true that all these questions ultimately hang together, and that no complete solution will be found for any one of them until the whole problem of our moral relation towards the lower animals is studied with far greater comprehensiveness.

For this reason it is perhaps unscientific to assert that any particular form of cruelty to animals is *worse* than another form; the truth is, that each of these hydra-heads, the offspring of one parent stem, has its own proper characteristic, and is different, not worse or better than the rest. To flesh-eating belongs the proud distinction of causing a greater bulk of animal suffering than any other habit whatsoever; to sport, the meed of unique and unparalleled brutality; while the patrons of murderous millinery afford the most marvellous instance of the capacity the human mind possesses for ignoring its personal responsibilities. To re-apply Keats's words:

> " For them the Ceylon diver held his breath,
> And went all naked to the hungry shark;
> For them his ears gush'd blood; for them in death
> The seal on the cold ice with piteous bark
> Lay full of darts; for them alone did seethe
> A thousand men in troubles wide and dark;
> Half ignorant, they turn'd an easy wheel,
> That set sharp racks at work, to pinch and peel."

CHAPTER VII

EXPERIMENTAL TORTURE

GREAT is the change when we turn from the easy thoughtless indifferentism of the sportsman or the milliner to the more determined and deliberately chosen attitude of the scientist—so great, indeed, that by many people, even among professed champions of animals' rights, it is held impossible to trace such dissimilar lines of action to one and the same source. Yet it can be shown, I think, that in this instance, as in those already examined, the prime cause of man's injustice to the lower animals is the belief that they are mere automata, devoid alike of spirit, character, and individuality ; only, while the ignorant sportsman expresses this contempt through the medium of the battue, and the milliner through that of the bonnet, the more seriously-minded physiologist works his work in the "experimental torture" of the laboratory. The difference lies in the temperament of the men, and in the tone of their profession; but in their denial of the most elementary rights of the lower races, they are all inspired and instigated by one common prejudice.

The analytical method employed by modern science tends ultimately, in the hands of its most enlightened exponents, to the recognition of a close relationship between mankind and the animals; but incidentally it has exercised a most sinister effect on the study of the *jus animalium* among the mass of average men. For consider the dealings of the so-called naturalist with the animals whose nature he makes it his business to observe! In ninety-nine cases out of a hundred, he is wholly unappreciative of the essential distinctive quality, the individuality, of the subject of his investigations, and becomes nothing more than a contented accumulator of facts, an industrious dissector of carcases. "I think the most important requisite in describing an animal," says Thoreau, "is to be sure that you give its character and spirit, for in that you have, without error, the sum and effect of all its parts known and unknown. Surely the most important part of an animal is its *anima*, its vital spirit, on which is based its character and all the particulars by which it most concerns us. Yet most scientific books which treat of animals leave this out altogether, and what they describe are, as it were, phenomena of dead matter."

The whole system of our "natural history" as practised at the present time, is based on this deplorably partial and misleading method. Does a rare bird alight on our shores? It is at once slaughtered by some enterprising collector, and proudly handed over to the nearest taxidermist, that it may be "preserved," among a number of other stuffed corpses, in the local "Museum." It is a dismal business at best, this science of the fowling-piece and the dissecting-knife, but it is in keeping with the materialistic tendency of a certain school of thought, and only a few of its professors rise out of it, and above it, to a maturer and more far-sighted understanding. "The child," says Michelet, "disports himself, shatters, and destroys; he finds his happiness in *undoing*. And science, in its childhood, does the same. It cannot study unless it kills. The sole use which it makes of a living mind is, in the first place, to dissect it. None carry into scientific pursuits that tender reverence for life which Nature rewards by unveiling to us her mysteries."

Experimental Torture

Under these circumstances, it is scarcely to be wondered at that modern scientists, their minds athirst for further and further opportunities of satisfying this analytical curiosity, should desire to have recourse to the experimental torture which is euphemistically described as "vivisection." They are caught and impelled by the overmastering passion of knowledge; and, as a handy subject for the gratification of this passion, they see before them the helpless race of animals, in part wild, in part domesticated, but alike regarded by the generality of mankind as incapable of possessing any "rights." They are practically accustomed (despite their ostensible disavowal of the Cartesian theory) to treat these animals as automata—things made to be killed and dissected and catalogued for the advancement of knowledge; they are, moreover, in their professional capacity, the lineal descendants of a class of men who, however kindly and considerate in other respects, have never scrupled to subordinate the strongest promptings of humaneness to the least of the supposed interests of science.[1] Given these conditions, it

[1] Vivisection is an ancient usage, having been practised for 2,000 years or more, in Egypt, Italy, and elsewhere. Human vivisection is mentioned by Galen

seems as inevitable that the physiologist should vivisect as that the country gentleman should shoot. Experimental torture is as appropriately the study of the half-enlightened man as sport is the amusement of the half-witted.

But the fact that vivisection is not, as some of its opponents would appear to regard it, a portentous, unaccountable phenomenon, but rather the logical outcome of a certain ill-balanced habit of mind, does not in any way detract from its intellectual and moral loathsomeness. It is idle to spend a single moment in advocating the rights of the lower animals, if such rights do not include a total and unqualified exemption from the awful tortures of vivisection—from the doom of being slowly

---

as having been fashionable for centuries before his day, and Celsus informs us that " they procured criminals out of prison, and, dissecting them alive, contemplated, while they were yet breathing, what nature had before concealed." The sorcerers, too, of the Middle Ages tortured both human beings and animals, with a view to the discovery of their medicinal elixirs. The recognition of the rights of men has now made human vivisection criminal, and the scientific inquisition of the present time counts animals alone as its victims. And here the Act of 1876 has fortunately, though not sufficiently, restricted the powers of the vivisector in this country.

Experimental Torture

and mercilessly dismembered, or flayed, or baked alive, or infected with some deadly virus, or subjected to any of the numerous modes of torture inflicted by the Scientific Inquisition. Let us heartily endorse the words of Miss Cobbe on this crucial subject, that "the *minimum* of all possible rights plainly is —to be spared the worst of all possible wrongs; and if a horse or dog have no claim to be spared from being maddened and mangled after the fashion of Pasteur and Chauveau, then it is impossible it can have any right at all, or that any offence against it, by gentle or simple, can deserve punishment."

It is necessary to speak strongly and unmistakably on this point, because, as I have already said, there is a disposition on the part of some of the "friends of animals" to palter and compromise with vivisection, as if the alleged "utility" of its practices, or the "conscientious" motives of its professors, put it on an altogether different footing from other kinds of inhumanity. "Much against my own feelings," wrote one of these backsliders,[1] "I do see a warrant for vivisection in the case of harmful animals, and animals which are

[1] "The Rights of an Animal," by E. B. Nicholson, 1879.

man's rivals for food. If an animal is doomed to be killed on other grounds, the vivisector, when its time comes, may step in, buy it, kill it in his own way, and take without self-reproach the gain to knowledge which he can get from its death. And my 'sweet is life' theory would further allow of animals being specially bred for vivisection—where and where only they would otherwise not have been bred at all." This astounding argument, which assumes the necessity of vivisection, gives away, it will be observed, the whole case of animals' rights.

The assertion, commonly made by the apologists of the Scientific Inquisition, that vivisection is justified by its utility—that it is, in fact, indispensable to the advance of knowledge and civilization [1]—is founded on a mere

---

[1] The medical argument of "utility" has always been held *in terrorem* over the unscientific assertion of animals' rights. Porphyry, writing in the third century, quotes the following from Claudius the Neapolitan, author of a treatise against abstinence from animal food. " How many will be prevented from having their diseases cured, if animals are abstained from! For we see that those who are blind recover their sight by eating a viper." Some of the results that scientists "see" nowadays may appear equally strange to posterity!

half-view of the position; the scientist, as I have already remarked, is a half-enlightened man. Let us assume (a large assumption, certainly, controverted as it is by some most weighty medical testimony) that the progress of surgical science is assisted by the experiments of the vivisector. What then? Before rushing to the conclusion that vivisection is justifiable on that account, a wise man will take into full consideration the other, the moral side of the question—the hideous injustice of torturing an innocent animal, and the terrible wrong thereby done to the humane sense of the community.

The wise scientist and the wise humanist are identical. A true science cannot possibly ignore the solid incontrovertible fact, that the practice of vivisection is revolting to the human conscience, even among the ordinary members of a not over-sensitive society. The so-called "science" (we are compelled unfortunately, in common parlance, to use the word in this specialized technical meaning) which deliberately overlooks this fact, and confines its view to the material aspects of the problem, is not science at all, but a one-sided assertion of the views which find favour with a particular class of men.

Nothing is necessary which is abhorrent, revolting, intolerable, to the general instincts of humanity. Better a thousand times that science should forego or postpone the questionable advantage of certain problematical discoveries, than that the moral conscience of the community should be unmistakably outraged by the confusion of right and wrong. The short cut is not always the right path; and to perpetrate a cruel injustice on the lower animals, and then attempt to excuse it on the ground that it will benefit posterity, is an argument which is as irrelevant as it is immoral. Ingenious it may be (in the way of hoodwinking the unwary) but it is certainly in no true sense scientific.

If there be one bright spot, one refreshing oasis, in the discussion of this dreary subject, it is the humorous recurrence of the old threadbare fallacy of "better for the animals themselves." Yes, even here, in the laboratory of the vivisector, amidst the baking and sawing and dissection, we are sometimes met by that familiar friend—the proud plea of a single-hearted regard for the interests of the suffering animals! Who knows but what some beneficent experimentalist, if only he be permitted to cut up a sufficient number of victims, may discover some potent remedy for all the lamented ills of the animal as well as of the human creation? Can we doubt that the victims themselves, if once they could realize the noble object of their martyrdom, would vie with each other in rushing eagerly on the knife? The only marvel is that, where the cause is so meritorious, no *human* volunteer has as yet come forward to die under the hands of the vivisector![1]

It is fully admitted that experiments on men would be far more valuable and conclusive than experiments on animals; yet scientists usually disavow any wish to revive these practices, and indignantly deny the rumours, occasionally circulated, that the poorer patients in hospitals are the subjects of such anatomical curiosity. Now here, it will be observed, in the case of men, the *moral* aspect of vivisection is admitted by the scientist as a matter of course, yet in the case of animals it is allowed no weight

[1] It is true, however, that Lord Aberdare, in presiding over the last annual meeting of the Royal Society for the Prevention of Cruelty to Animals, and in warning the society against entering on an anti-vivisection crusade, gave utterance to the delightfully comical remark that he had himself been thrice operated on, and was all the better for it!

whatever! How can this strange inconsistency be justified, unless on the assumption that men have rights, but animals have no rights—in other words, that animals are mere *things*, possessed of no purpose, and no claim on the justice and forbearance of the community?

One of the most notable and ominous features in the apologies offered for vivisection is the assertion, so commonly made by scientific writers, that it is "no worse" than certain kindred practices. When the upholders of any accused institution begin to plead that it is "no worse" than other institutions, we may feel quite assured that the case is a very bad one indeed—it is the drowning man catching at the last straw and shred of argument. Thus the advocates of experimental torture are reduced to the expedient of laying stress on the cruelties of the butcher and the herdsman, and inquiring why, if pole-axing and castration are permissible, vivisection may not also be permitted.[1] Sport, also, is a practice which has greatly shocked the susceptibilities of the humane vivisector. A writer in the "Fortnightly Review" has defined sport as

[1] See J. Cotter Morrison's article on "Scientific *versus* Bucolic Vivisection," "Fortnightly Review," 1885.

Experimental Torture

"the love of the clever destruction of living things," and has calculated that three millions of animals are yearly mangled by English sportsmen, in addition to those killed outright."[1]

Now if the attack on vivisection emanated primarily or wholly from the apologists of the sportsman and slaughterer, this *tu quoque* of the scientist's must be allowed to be a smart, though rather flippant, retort; but when *all* cruelty is arraigned as inhuman and unjustifiable, an evasive answer of this kind ceases to have any relevancy or pertinence. Let us admit, however, that, in contrast with the childish brutality of the sportsman, the undoubted seriousness and conscientiousness of the vivisector (for I do not question that he acts from conscientious motives) may be counted to his advantage. But then we have to remember, on the other hand, that the conscientious man, when he goes wrong, is far more dangerous to society than the knave or the fool; indeed, the special horror of vivisection consists precisely in this fact, that it is not due to mere thoughtlessness and ignorance, but represents a deliberate, avowed, conscientious invasion of the very principle of animals' rights.

I have already said that it is idle to specu-

[1] Professor Jevons, "Fortnightly Review," 1876.

late which is the worst form of cruelty to animals, for certainly in this subject, if anywhere, we must "reject the lore of nicely calculated less or more." Vivisection, if there be any truth at all in the principle for which I am contending, is not the root, but the fine flower and consummation of barbarity and injustice—the *ne plus ultra* of iniquity in man's dealings with the lower races. The root of the evil lies, as I have throughout asserted, in that detestable assumption (detestable equally whether it be based on pseudo-religious or pseudo-scientific grounds) that there is a gulf, an impassable barrier, between man and the animals, and that the moral instincts of compassion, justice, and love, are to be as sedulously repressed and thwarted in the one direction as they are to be fostered and extended in the other.

For this very reason our crusade against the Scientific Inquisition, to be thorough and successful, must be founded on the rock of consistent opposition to cruelty in every form and phase; it is useless to denounce vivisection as the source of all inhumanities, and, while demanding its immediate suppression, to suppose that other minor questions may be indefinitely postponed. It is true that the actual emancipation of the lower races, as of the human, can only proceed step by step, and that it is both natural and politic to strike first at what is most repulsive to the public conscience. I am not depreciating the wisdom of such a concentration of effort on any particular point, but warning my readers against the too common tendency to forget the general principle that underlies each individual protest.

The spirit in which we approach these matters should be a liberal and far-seeing one. Those who work for the abolition of vivisection, or any other particular wrong, should do so with the avowed purpose of capturing one stronghold of the enemy, not because they believe that the war will then be over, but because they will be able to use the position thus gained as an advantageous starting-point for still further progression.

CHAPTER VIII

LINES OF REFORM

HAVING now applied the principle with which we started to the several cases where it appears to be most flagrantly overlooked, we are in a better position to estimate the difficulties and the possibilities of its future acceptance. Our investigation of animals' rights has necessarily been, in large measure, an enumeration of animals' wrongs, a story of cruelty and injustice which might have been unfolded in far greater and more impressive detail, had there been any reason for here repeating what has been elsewhere established by other writers beyond doubt or dispute.

But my main purpose was to deal with a general theory rather than with particular instances; and enough has already been said to show that while man has much cause to be grateful to the lower animals for the innumerable services rendered by them, he can hardly pride himself on the record of the counter-benefits which they have received at his hands. "If we consider," says Primatt, "the excruciating injuries offered on our part to the brutes, and the patience on their part; how frequent *our* provocation, and how seldom *their* resentment (and in some cases *our* weakness and *their* strength, *our* slowness and *their* swiftness) one would be almost tempted to suppose that the brutes had combined in one general scheme of benevolence, to teach mankind lessons of mercy and meekness by their own forbearance and longsuffering."

It is unwise, no doubt, to dwell too exclusively on the wrongs of which animals are the victims; it is still more unwise to ignore them as they are to-day ignored by the large majority of mankind. It is full time that this question were examined in the light of some rational and guiding principle, and that we ceased to drift helplessly between the extremes of total indifference on the one hand, and spasmodic, partially-applied compassion on the other. We have had enough, and too much, of trifling with this or that isolated aspect of the subject, and of playing off the exposure of somebody else's insensibility by way of a balance for our own, as if a *tu quoque* were a sufficient justification of a man's moral delinquencies.

The terrible sufferings that are quite needlessly inflicted on the lower animals under the plea of domestic usage, food-demands, sport, fashion, and science, are patent to all who have the seeing eye and the feeling heart to apprehend them; those sufferings will not be lessened, nor will man's responsibility be diminished by any such irrelevant assertions as that vivisection is less cruel than sport, or sport less cruel than butchering,—nor yet by the contrary contention that vivisection, or sport, or flesh-eating, as the case may be, is the one prime origin of all human inhumanity. We want a comprehensive principle which will cover all these varying instances, and determine the true lines of reform.

Such a principle, as I have throughout insisted, can only be found in the recognition of the right of animals, as of men, to be exempt from any unnecessary suffering or serfdom, the right to live a natural life of "restricted freedom," subject to the real, not supposed or pretended, requirements of the general community. It may be said, and with truth, that the perilous vagueness of the word "necessary" must leave a convenient loop-hole of escape to anyone who wishes to justify his own treatment of animals, however unjustifiable that treatment may appear; the vivisector will assert that his practice is necessary in the interests of science, the flesh-eater that he cannot maintain his health without animal food, and so on through the whole category of systematic oppression.

The difficulty is an inevitable one. No form of words can be devised for the expression of rights, human or animal, which is not liable to some sort of evasion; and all that can be done is to fix the responsibility of deciding between what is necessary and unnecessary, between factitious personal wants and genuine social demands, on those in whom is vested the power of exacting the service or sacrifice required. The appeal being thus made, and the issue thus stated, it may be confidently trusted that the personal conscience of individuals and the public conscience of the nation, acting and reacting in turn on each other, will slowly and surely work out the only possible solution of this difficult and many-sided problem.

For that the difficulties involved in this animal question are many and serious, no one, I imagine, would dispute, and certainly no attempt has been made or will be made, in this essay to minimise or deny them.[1] It may suit the purpose of those who would retard all humanitarian progress to represent its advocates as mere dreamers and sentimentalists—men and women who befool themselves by shutting their eyes to the fierce struggle that is everywhere being waged in the world of nature, while they point with virtuous indignation to the iniquities perpetrated by man. But it is possible to be quite free from any such sentimental illusions, and yet to hold a very firm belief in the principle of animals' rights. We do not deny, or attempt to explain away, the existence of evil in nature, or the fact that the life of the lower races, as of mankind, is based to a large degree on rapine and violence; nor can we pretend to say whether this evil will ever be wholly amended. It is therefore confessedly impossible, at the present time, to formulate an entirely and logically consistent philosophy of rights; but that would be a poor argument against grappling with the subject at all.

The hard unmistakable facts of the situation, when viewed in their entirety, are not by any means calculated to inspire with confidence the

[1] See p. 22.

opponents of humane reform. For, if it be true that internecine competition is a great factor in the economy of nature, it is no less true, as has been already pointed out,[1] that co-operation is also a great factor therein. Furthermore, though there are many difficulties besetting the onward path of humanitarianism, an even greater difficulty has to be faced by those who refuse to proceed along that path, viz., the fact —as strong a fact as any that can be produced on the other side—that the instinct of compassion and justice to the lower animals has already been so largely developed in the human conscience as to obtain legislative recognition. If the theory of animals' rights is a mere idealistic phantasy, it follows that we have long ago committed ourselves to a track which can lead us no whither. Is it then proposed that we should retrace our steps, with a view to regaining the antique position of savage and consistent callousness ; or are we to remain perpetually in our present meaningless attitude, admitting the moral value of a partially awakened sensibility, yet opposing an eternal *non possumus* to any further improvement ? Neither of these alternatives is for a moment conceivable ; it is perfectly certain

[1] See p. 26.

that there will still be a forward movement, and along the same lines as in the past.

Nor need we be at all disconcerted by the derisive enquiries of our antagonists as to the final outcome of such theories. "There is some reason to hope," said the author of the ironical "Vindication of the Rights of Brutes," "that this essay will soon be followed by treatises on the rights of vegetables and minerals, and that thus the doctrine of perfect equality will become universal." To which suggestion we need only answer, "Perhaps." It is for each age to initiate its own ethical reforms, according to the light and sensibility of its own instincts; further and more abstruse questions, at present insoluble, may safely be left to the more mature judgment of posterity. The human conscience furnishes the safest and simplest indicator in these matters. We know that certain acts of injustice affect us as they did not affect our forefathers—it is our duty to set these right. It is not our duty to agitate problems, which, at the present date, excite no unmistakable moral feeling.

The humane instinct will assuredly continue to develope. And it should be observed that to advocate the rights of animals is far more than to plead for compassion or justice to-

Lines of Reform

wards the victims of ill-usage; it is not only, and not primarily, for the sake of the victims that we plead, but for the sake of mankind itself. Our true civilisation, our race-progress, our *humanity* (in the best sense of the term) are concerned in this development; it is ourselves, our own vital instincts, that we wrong, when we trample on the rights of the fellow-beings, human or animal, over whom we chance to hold jurisdiction. It has been admirably said [1] that, " terrible as is the lot of the subjects of cruelty and injustice, that of the perpetrators is even worse, by reason of the debasement and degradation of character implied and incurred. For the principles of Humanity cannot be renounced with impunity; but their renunciation, if persisted in, involves inevitably the forfeiture of Humanity itself. And to cease through such forfeiture to be man is to become demon."

This most important point is constantly overlooked by the opponents of humanitarian reform. They labour, unsuccesssfully enough, to minimise the complaints of animals' wrongs, on the plea that these wrongs, though great, are not so great as they are represented to be,

[1] Edward Maitland; Address to the Humanitarian League.

and that in any case it is not possible, or not urgently desirable, for man to alleviate them. As if *human* interests also were not intimately bound up in every such compassionate endeavour! The case against injustice to animals stands, in this respect, on exactly the same grounds as that against injustice to man, and may be illustrated by some suggestive words of De Quincey's on the typical subject of corporal punishment. This practice, he remarks, "is usually argued with a single reference to the case of him who suffers it; and *so* argued, God knows that it is worthy of all abhorrence: but the weightiest argument against it is the foul indignity which is offered to our common nature lodged in the person of him on whom it is inflicted."

And this brings us back to the moral of the whole matter. The idea of Humanity is no longer confined to man; it is beginning to extend itself to the lower animals, as in the past it has been gradually extended to savages and slaves. "Behold the animals. There is not one but the human soul lurks within it, fulfilling its destiny as surely as within you." So writes the author of "Towards Democracy;" and what has long been felt by the poet is now being scientifically corroborated

Lines of Reform

by the anthropologist and philosopher. "The standpoint of modern thought," says Büchner,[1] "no longer recognises in animals a difference of kind, but only a difference of degree, and sees the principle of intelligence developing through an endless and unbroken series."

It is noteworthy that, on this point, evolutionary science finds itself in agreement with oriental tradition. "The doctrine of metempsychosis," says Strauss,[2] "knits men and beasts together here [in the East], and unites the whole of Nature in one sacred and mysterious bond. The breach between the two was opened in the first place by Judaism, with its hatred of the Gods of Nature, next by the dualism of Christianity. It is remarkable that at present a deeper sympathy with the animal world should have arisen among the more civilized nations, which manifests itself here and there in societies for the prevention of cruelty to animals. It is thus apparent that what on the one hand is the product of modern science —the giving up of the spiritualistic isolation of man from Nature—reveals itself simultaneously through the channel of popular sentiment."

[1] "Mind in Animals," translated by Annie Besant.
[2] "The Old Faith and the New," translated by Mathilde Blind.

It is not human life only that is lovable and sacred, but *all* innocent and beautiful life : the great republic of the future will not confine its beneficence to man. The isolation of man from Nature, by our persistent culture of the ratiocinative faculty, and our persistent neglect of the instinctive, has hitherto been the penalty we have had to pay for our incomplete and partial "civilization ;" there are many signs that the tendency will now be towards that "Return to Nature" of which Rousseau was the prophet. But let it not for a moment be supposed that an acceptance of the gospel of Nature implies an abandonment or depreciation of intellect—on the contrary, it is the assertion that reason itself can never be at its best, can never be truly rational, except when it is in perfect harmony with the deep-seated emotional instincts and sympathies which underlie all thought.

The true scientist and humanist is he who will reconcile brain to heart, and show us how, without any sacrifice of what we have gained in knowledge, we may resume what we have temporarily lost during the process of acquiring that knowledge—the sureness of intuitive faculty which is originally implanted in men and animals alike. Only by this return

Lines of Reform

to the common fount of feeling will it be possible for man to place himself in right relationship towards the lower animals, and to break down the fatal barrier of antipathy that he has himself erected. If we contrast the mental and moral attitude of the generality of mankind towards the lower races with that of such men as St. Francis or Thoreau, we see what far-reaching possibilities still lie before us on this line of development, and what an immense extension is even now waiting to be given to our most advanced ideas of social unity and brotherhood.

I have already remarked on the frequent and not altogether unjustifiable complaint against "lovers of animals," that they are often indifferent to the struggle for human rights, while they concern themselves so eagerly over the interests of the lower races. Equally true is the converse statement, that many earnest reformers and philanthropists, men who have a genuine passion for human liberty and progress, are coldly sceptical or even bitterly hostile on the subject of the rights of animals. This organic limitation of sympathies must be recognised and regretted, but it is worse than useless for the one class of reformers to indulge in blame or recrimination against the other. It is certain that they are both working towards the same ultimate end; and if they cannot actually co-operate, they may at least refrain from unnecessarily thwarting and opposing each other.

The principles of justice, if they are to make solid and permanent headway, must be applied with thoroughness and consistency. If there are rights of animals, there must *a fortiori* be rights of men; and, as I have shown, it is impossible to maintain that an admission of human rights does not involve an admission of animals' rights also. Now it may not always fall to the lot of the same persons to advocate both kinds of rights, but these rights are, nevertheless, being simultaneously and concurrently advocated; and those who are in a position to take a clear and wide survey of the whole humanitarian movement are aware that its final success is dependent on this broad onward tendency. "Man will not be truly man," says Michelet, "until he shall labour seriously for that which the earth expects from him—the pacification and harmonious union of all living Nature."

The advent of democracy, imperfect though any democracy must be which does not embrace all living things within its scope, will be

Lines of Reform

of enormous assistance to the cause of animals' rights, for under the present unequal and inequitable social system there is no possibility of those claims receiving their due share of attention. In the rush and hurry of a competitive society, where commercial profit is avowed to be the main object of work, and where the well-being of men and women is ruthlessly sacrificed to that object, what likelihood is there that the lower animals will not be used with a sole regard to the same predominant purpose? Humane individuals may here and there protest, and the growing conscience of the public may express itself in legislation against the worst forms of palpable ill-usage, but the bulk of the people simply cannot, and will not, afford to treat animals as they ought to be treated. Do the wealthy classes show any such consideration? Let "amateur butchery" and "murderous millinery" be the answer. Can it be wondered, then, that the "lower classes," whose own rights are existent far more in theory than in fact, should exhibit a feeling of stolid indifference to the rights of the still lower animals?

It has been said that, "If in a mob of Londoners, Parisians, New Yorkers, Berliners, Melbourners, a dove fluttered down to seek a refuge, a hundred dirty hands would be stretched out to seize it, and wring its neck; and if anyone tried to save and cherish it, he would be rudely bonneted, and mocked, and hustled amidst the brutal guffaws of roughs, lower and more hideous in aspect and in nature than any animal which lives."[1] This may be so; yet it must be remembered that it is not the people, but the lords, who have hitherto prevented the suppression, in England at any rate, of the infamous pastime of pigeon-shooting. It is to the democracy, and the democratic sense of kinship and brotherhood, extending first to mankind, and then to the lower races, that we must look for future progress. The emancipation of men will bring with it another and still wider emancipation—of animals.

In conclusion, we are brought face to face with this practical problem—by what immediate means can we best provide for the attainment of the end we have in view? What are the surest remedies for the present wrongs, and the surest pledges for the future rights, of the victims of human supremacy? The answer, I think, must be that there are two pre-eminently important methods which are some-

[1] Ouida, "Fortnightly Review," April, 1892.

times regarded as contradictory in principle, but which, as I hope to show, are not only quite compatible, but even mutually serviceable and to some degree inter-dependent. We have no choice but to work by one or the other of these methods, and, if we are wise, we shall endeavour to work by both simultaneously, using the first as our chief instrument of reform, the second as an auxiliary and supplementary instrument. The two methods to which I allude are the educational and the legislative.

I. Education, in the largest sense of the term, has always been, and must always remain, the antecedent and indispensable condition of humanitarian progress. Very excellent are the words of John Bright on the subject (let us forget for the nonce that he was an angler). " Humanity to animals is a great point. If I were a teacher in a school, I would make it a very important part of my business to impress every boy and girl with the duty of his or her being kind to all animals. It is impossible to say how much suffering there is in the world from the barbarity or unkindness which people show to what we call the inferior creatures."

It may be doubted, however, whether the

young will ever be specially impressed with the lesson of humanity as long as the general tone of their elders and instructors is one of cynical indifference, if not of absolute hostility, to the recognition of animals' rights.[1] It is society as a whole, and not one class in particular, that needs enlightenment and remonstrance; in fact, the very conception and scope of what is known as a "liberal education" must be revolutionized and extended. For if we find fault with the narrow and unscientific spirit of what is known as "science," we must in fairness admit that our academic "humanities," the *literæ humaniores* of colleges and schools, together with much of our modern culture and refinement, are scarcely less deficient in that quickening spirit of sympathetic brotherhood, without which all the accomplishments that the mind of man can devise are as the borrowed cloak of an imperfectly realized civilization, assumed by some barbarous tribe but half emerged from savagery. This divorce of "humanism" from humaneness is one of

[1] "They tell children, perhaps, that they must not be cruel to animals . . . . what avails all the fine talk about morality, in contrast with acts of barbarism and immorality presented to them on all sides?"—GUSTAV VON STRUVE.

Lines of Reform

the subtlest dangers by which society is beset; for, if we grant that love needs to be tempered and directed by wisdom, still more needful is it that wisdom should be informed and vitalized by love.

It is therefore not only our children who need to be educated in the proper treatment of animals, but our scientists, our religionists, our moralists, and our men of letters. For in spite of the vast progress of humanitarian ideas during the present century, it must be confessed that the popular exponents of western thought [1] are still for the most part quite unable to appreciate the profound truth of those words of Rousseau, which should form the basis of an enlightened system of

---

[1] Eastern thought has always been far humaner than western, however deplorably in the East also practice may lag behind profession. In an interesting book lately published ("Man and Beast in India," by J. Lockwood Kipling), an extremely unfavourable account is given of the Hindoo treatment of animals. The alleged kindness of the natives, says the author, is nothing better than "a vague reluctance to take life by a sudden positive act," and "does not preserve the ox, the horse, and the ass from being unmercifully beaten, over-driven, over-laden, under-fed, and worked with sores under their harness." But he admits that "a more humane temper prevails with regard to free creatures than in the west."

instruction: " Hommes, soyez humains ! C'est votre premier devoir. Quelle sagesse y a-t-il pour vous, hors de l'humanité ? "

But how is this vast educational change to be inaugurated—let alone accomplished? Like all far-reaching reforms which are promoted by a few believers in the face of the public indifferentism, it can only be carried through by the energy and resolution of its supporters. The efforts which the various humane societies are now making in special directions, each concentrating its attack on a particular abuse, must be supplemented and strengthened by a crusade—an intellectual, literary, and social crusade—against the central cause of oppression, viz.: the disregard of the natural kinship between man and the animals, and the consequent denial of their rights. We must insist on having the whole question fully considered and candidly discussed, and must no longer permit its most important issues to be shirked because it does not suit the convenience or the prejudices of comfortable folk to give attention to them.

Above all, the sense of ridicule that at present attaches to the supposed "sentimentalism" of an advocacy of animals' rights must be faced and swept away. The fear of this

Lines of Reform 123

absurd charge deprives the cause of humanity of many workers who would otherwise lend their aid, and accounts in part for the unduly diffident and apologetic tone which is too often adopted by humanitarians. We must meet this ridicule, and retort it without hesitation on those to whom it properly pertains. The laugh must be turned against the true "cranks" and "crotchet-mongers"—the noodles who can give no wiser reason for the infliction of suffering on animals than that it is "better for the animals themselves"—the flesh-eaters who labour under the pious belief that animals were "sent" us as food—the silly women who imagine that the corpse of a bird is a becoming article of head-gear—the half-witted sportsmen who vow that the vigour of the English race is dependent on the practice of fox-hunting— and the half-enlightened scientists who are unaware that vivisection has moral and spiritual, no less than physical, consequences. That many of our arguments are mere superficial sword-play, and do not touch the profound emotional sympathies on which the cause of humanity rests, is a fact which does not lessen their controversial significance. For this is a case where those who take the sword shall perish by the sword ; and the clever men-of-the-world who twit consistent humanitarians with sickly sentimentality may perhaps discover that they themselves—fixed as they are in an ambiguous and utterly untenable position—are the sickliest sentimentalists of all.

II. Legislation, where the protection of harmless animals is concerned, is the fit supplement and sequel to education, and the objections urged against it are for the most part unreasonable. It must inevitably fail in its purpose, say some; for how can the mere passing of a penal statute prevent the innumerable unwitnessed acts of cruelty and oppression which make up the great total of animal suffering? But the purpose of legislation is not merely thus preventive. Legislation is the record, the register, of the moral sense of the community; it follows, not precedes, the development of that moral sense, but nevertheless in its turn reacts on it, strengthens it, and secures it against the danger of retrocession. It is well that society should proclaim, formally and decisively, its abhorrence of certain practices; and I do not think it can be doubted, by those who have studied the history of the movement, that the general treatment of domestic animals in this country, bad as it still is, would be infinitely worse at this day but for the progressive and punitive legislation that dates from the passing of "Martin's Act" in 1822.

The further argument, so commonly advanced, that "force is no remedy," and that it is better to trust to the good feeling of mankind than to impose a legal restriction, is an amiable criticism which might doubtless be applied with great effect to a large majority of our existing penal enactments, but it is not very applicable to the case under discussion. For if force is ever allowable, surely it is so when it is applied for a strictly *defensive* purpose, such as to safeguard the weak and helpless from violence and aggression. The protection of animals by statute marks but another step onward in that course of humanitarian legislation which, among numerous triumphs, has abolished slavery and passed the Factory Acts— always in the teeth of this same time-honoured but irrelevant objection that "force is no remedy." Equally fatuous is the assertion that the administrators of the law cannot be trusted to adjudicate between master and "beast." It was long ago stated by Lord Erskine that "to distinguish the severest discipline, for enforcing activity and commanding obedience in such dependents, from brutal ferocity and cruelty, never yet puzzled a judge or jury—never, at least, in my long experience."

Such arguments against the legal protection of animals were admirably refuted by John Stuart Mill. " The reasons for legal intervention in favour of children," he said, " apply not less strongly to the case of those unfortunate slaves and victims of the most brutal part of mankind, the lower animals. It is by the grossest misunderstanding of the principles of Liberty that the infliction of exemplary punishment on ruffianism practised towards these defenceless beings has been treated as a meddling by Government with things beyond its province—an interference with domestic life. The domestic life of domestic tyrants is one of the things which it is most imperative on the Law to interfere with. And it is to be regretted that metaphysical scruples respecting the nature and source of the authority of governments should induce many warm supporters of laws against cruelty to the lower animals to seek for justification of such laws in the incidental consequences of the indulgence of ferocious habits to the interest of human beings, rather than in the intrinsic merits of the thing itself. What it would be the duty of a human being, possessed of the

Lines of Reform

requisite physical strength, to prevent by force, if attempted in his presence, it cannot be less incumbent on society generally to repress. The existing laws of England are chiefly defective in the trifling—often almost nominal—maximum to which the penalty, even in the worst cases, is limited."[1]

Let us turn now to the practical politics of the question, and consider in what instances we may suitably appeal for further legislative recognition of the rights of animals. Admitting that education must always precede law, and that we can only make penal those offences which are already condemned by the better feeling of the nation, we are still bound to point out that in several particulars there is now urgent need of bringing the lagging influence of the legislature into a line with a rapidly advancing public opinion. It is possible that, in some cases, certain prevalent cruelties might be suppressed, without any change in the law, by magistrates and juries giving a wider interpretation to the rather vague wording of the existing statutes. If this cannot be done, the statutes themselves should be amended, so as to meet the larger require-

[1] "Principles of Political Economy."

ments of a more enlightened national conscience.

There are not a few cruel practices, in common vogue at the present day, which are every whit as strongly condemned by thinking people as were bull-baiting and cock-fighting at the time of their prohibition in 1835. Foremost among these practices, because supported by the sanction of the State and carried on in the Queen's name, is the institution of the Royal Buckhounds.[1] It does not seem too much to demand that all worrying of tame or captured animals—whether of the stag turned out from a cart, the rabbit from a sack, or the pigeon from a cage—should be interpreted as equivalent to "baiting," and so brought within the scope of the Acts of 1835 and 1849. There is also need of extending to "vermin" some sort of protection against the wholly unnecessary tortures that are recklessly inflicted on them, and of abolishing or restricting the common use of the barbarous steel-trap.

The exposure lately made[2] of the horrors of Atlantic cattle-ships—scenes that reproduce almost exactly the worst atrocities of the slaver—is likely to lead to some welcome improve-

[1] See p. 74.
[2] "Cattle-Ships," by Samuel Plimsoll, 1890.

Lines of Reform

ment in the details of that lugubrious traffic. But this will not be sufficient in itself; for the cruelties committed in the slaughter, no less than in the transit, of "live-stock" call imperatively for some public cognizance and reprobation. The discontinuance, in our crowded districts, of all private slaughter-houses, and the substitution of public abattoirs under efficient municipal control, would do something to mitigate the worst features of the evil, and this reform should at once be pressed on the attention of local legislative bodies. Lastly, in this short list of urgent temporary measures, stands the question of vivisection; and here there can be no relaxation of the demand for total and unqualified prohibition.

But, when all is said, it remains true that legislation, important though it is, must ever be secondary to the awakening of the humane instincts; even education itself can only appeal with success to those whose minds are in some degree naturally predisposed to receive it. I have spoken of the desirability of an intellectual crusade against the main causes of the unjust treatment of animals; but I would not be understood to believe, as some humanitarians appear to do, that a hardened world might be miraculously converted by the preaching of a new St. Francis, if such a personality could be somehow evolved out of our nineteenth-century commercialism![1] In this infinitely complex modern society, great wrongs cannot be wholly righted by simple means, not even by the consuming enthusiasm of the prophet; since any particular form of injustice is but part and parcel of a far more deep-lying evil —the selfish, aggressive tendencies that are still so largely inherent in the human race.

Only with the gradual progress of an enlightened sense of equality shall we remedy these wrongs; and the object of our crusade should be not so much to convert opponents (who, by the very disabilities and limitations of their faculties, can never be really converted,) as to set the confused problem in a clear light, and at least discriminate unmistakably between our enemies and our allies. In all social controversies the issues are greatly obscured by the babel of names and phrases and cross-arguments that are bandied to and fro; so that many persons, who by natural sympathy and inclination are the friends of reform, are found to be ranked among its foes; while not

[1] See article by Ouida, "Fortnightly Review," April, 1892.

Lines of Reform

a few of its foes, in similar unconsciousness, have strayed into the opposite camp. To state the issues distinctly, and so attract and consolidate a genuine body of support, is, perhaps, at the present time, the best service that humanitarians can render to the movement they wish to promote.

In conclusion, I would state emphatically that this essay is not an appeal *ad misericordiam* to those who themselves practise, or who condone in others, the deeds against which a protest is here raised. It is not a plea for "mercy" (save the mark!) to the "brute-beasts" whose sole criminality consists in not belonging to the noble family of *homo sapiens*. It is addressed rather to those who see and feel that, as has been well said, "the great advancement of the world, throughout all ages, is to be measured by the increase of humanity and the decrease of cruelty"—that man, to be truly man, must cease to abnegate his common fellowship with all living nature—and that the coming realization of human rights will inevitably bring after it the tardier but not less certain realization of the rights of the lower races.

APPENDIX

THE TERM "RIGHTS"[1]

It was argued by Mr. D. G. Ritchie, in his book on "Natural Rights," that though "we may be said to have duties of *kindness towards* the animals," it is "incorrect to represent these as strictly *duties towards* the animals themselves, as if they had rights against us." (The italics are Mr. Ritchie's.) I take this to mean that, in man's "duty of kindness," it is the "kindness" only that has reference to animals, the "duty" being altogether the private affair of the man. The kindness is, so to speak, the water, and the duty is the tap; and the convenience of this arrangement is that the man can shut off the kindness whenever it suits him to do so; as, for example, it suited Mr. Ritchie in regard to the question of vivisection.

It is strange that ethical authorities should thus hold, as Catholic theologians do, that we owe no direct duties to animals, and that animals not being "persons" have, strictly speaking, no rights. Indeed, so entertaining did the very idea of the "personality" of animals appear to Mr. Ritchie that he waxed humorous in his desire to know whether a sponge is a "person" or "several persons," and

[1] *Animals' Rights* by Henry S. Salt, 1922.

whether the parasites on a dog are to be respected as "persons," and so forth.

On the other side, the humanitarian contention is quite clear—that there is no difference *in kind* between man and the other animals, nor any warrant in science or ethics for drawing between them, as between "persons" and "things," an absolute line of demarcation. Compelled to admit that the difference is only one of degree, Mr. Ritchie sought to evade the significance of this fact by arguing that it does not follow that, if men have rights, animals also have rights "in the same sense of the term." I maintain that it *does* so follow. If by the recognition of rights we mean that man, as a sentient and intelligent being, should be exempt from all avoidable suffering, it follows that other beings who are also sentient and intelligent, though in a lower degree, should have, in a lower degree, the same exemption. This principle, if pressed to its extreme logical conclusion, will of course lead, like all other principles, to what Mr. Ritchie called "difficult questions of casuistry," and will open a door for small jokes about the personality of parasites and sponges.

Then, again, it is too often overlooked that the rights claimed for animals, as for men, are not absolute but conditional ("this restricted freedom" is Herbert Spencer's expression), and that a recognition of the rights of other beings is not incompatible with an equal assertion of one's own. Self-defence is the first and most obvious right of everyone. If, for instance, we hold that a tiger has a right to be spared any unnecessary torture, are we compelled on that account to allow him to eat us if he comes out of his cage? And how would our shooting the tiger, under those untoward circumstances, prove that the tiger is not a "person," inasmuch as murderers and *human* tigers are similarly treated under similar conditions? This "tiger" argument, to which Professor Ritchie was much addicted, is really very small game.

1895.

BIBLIOGRAPHY[1]

I HAVE not attempted in the following pages to give a complete bibliography of the doctrine of Animals' Rights, but merely a list of the chief English works, touching directly on that subject, which have come within my own notice. The passages quoted from the older and less accessible books may serve the double purpose of showing the rise and progress of the movement, and of reinforcing the conclusions arrived at in the essay to which they are appended.

The Fable of the Bees. By Bernard de Mandeville. 1723.

As Mandeville, whether cynic or moralist, has been credited by some opponents of the rights of animals with being the author of that pernicious theory, I quote a few sentences from the most famous of his volumes: " I have often thought," he says, "if it was not for this tyranny which custom usurps over us, that men of any tolerable good-nature could never be reconcil'd to the killing of so many animals for their daily food, as long as the

[1] Comprising the bibliographies from the 1892 and 1922 editions of *Animals' Rights* by Henry S. Salt.

bountiful earth so plentifully provides them with varieties of vegetable dainties. . . . In such perfect animals as sheep and oxen, in whom the heart, the brain and nerves differ so little from ours, and in whom the separation of the spirits from the blood, the organs of sense, and consequently feeling itself, are the same as they are in human creatures; I can't imagine how a man not harden'd in blood and massacre is able to see a violent death, and the pangs of it, without concern. In answer to this, most people will think it sufficient to say that all things being allow'd to be made for the service of man, there can be no cruelty in putting creatures to the use they were design'd for; but I have heard men make this reply while their nature within them has reproach'd them with the falsehood of the assertion."

Free Thoughts upon the Brute Creation. By John Hildrop, M.A. London, 1742.

This "examination" of Father Bougeant's "Philosophical Amusement upon the Language of Beasts" (1740), in which it is ironically contended that the souls of animals are imprisoned devils, is an argument in favour of animal immortality, in the form of two letters addressed to a lady. "Do but examine your own compassionate heart," says the author, "and tell me, do you not think it a breach of natural justice wantonly and without necessity to torment, much more to take away the life of any creature, except for the preservation and happiness of your own being ; which, in our present state of enmity and discord, is sometimes unavoidable? . . . But I expect you will tell me, as many grave authors of great learning and little understanding have done before you, that there is not even the appearance of injustice or cruelty in this procedure ; that if the brutes themselves had power to speak, to complain, to appeal to a court of justice, and plead their own cause, they could have no just reason for such complaint. This you may say, but I know you too well to believe you think so; but it is an objection thrown in your way by some serious writers upon this subject. They tell you that their existence was given them upon this very condition, that it should be temporary and short, that after they had flutter'd, or crept, or swam, or walk'd about their respective elements for a little season, they should be swept away by the hand of violence, or the course of nature, into an entire extinction of being, to make room for their successors in the same circle of vanity and corruption. But, pray, who told them so? Where did they learn this philosophy? Does either reason or revelation give the least countenance to such a bold assertion? So far from it, that it seems a direct contradiction to both."

A Reasonable Plea for the Animal Creation. By Robert Morris, London, 1746.

A reprint of some letters urging that "we have no right to destroy, much less to eat of anything which has life."

An Essay on the Future Life of Brutes. By Richard Dean, Manchester, 1767.

The probability of a future life for animals is asserted on scriptural and other grounds.

An Apology for the Brute Creation, or Abuse of Animals Censured. By James Granger, London, 1772.

A short sermon condemning cruelty to animals in sport, etc.

A Dissertation on the Duty of Mercy and Sin of Cruelty to Brute Animals. By Humphry Primatt, D.D. London, 1776.

"However men may differ," says the author of this quaint but excellent book, "as to speculative points of religion, justice is a rule of universal extent and invariable obligation. We acknowledge this important truth in all matters in which Man is concerned, but then we limit it to our own species only. And though we are able to trace the most evident marks of the Creator's wisdom and goodness, in the formation and appointment of the various classes of animals that are inferior to men, yet the consciousness of our own dignity and excellence is apt to suggest to us that Man alone of all terrestrial animals is the only proper object of mercy and compassion, because he is the most highly favoured and distinguished. Misled with this prejudice in our own favour, we overlook some of the *Brutes* as if they were meer excrescences of Nature, beneath our notice and infinitely unworthy the care and cognizance of the Almighty ; and we consider others of them as made only for our service ; and so long as we can apply them to our use we are careless and indifferent as to their happiness or misery, and can hardly bring ourselves to suppose that there is any kind of *duty* incumbent upon us toward them. To rectify this mistaken notion is the design of this treatise."

With much force he applies to the animal question the precept of *doing to others as we would be done unto*. " If, in *brutal* shape, *we* had been endued with the same degree of reason and reflection which we now enjoy; and other beings, in *human* shape, should take upon them to torment, abuse, and barbarously ill-treat us, because we were not made in their shape ; the injustice and cruelty of their behaviour to us would be self-evident ; and we should naturally infer that, whether we walk upon two legs or four; whether our heads are prone or erect ; whether we are naked or covered

Appendix

with hair; whether we have tails or no tails, horns or no horns, long ears or round ears; or, whether we bray like an ass, speak like a man, whistle like a bird, or are mute as a fish—Nature never intended these distinctions as foundations for right of tyranny and oppression."

He exposes the fallacy of the argument drawn from the cruelty of animals to animals. "For us to infer that men may be cruel to brutes in general, because some brutes are naturally fierce and bloodthirsty, is tantamount to saying, Cruelty in Britain is no sin, because there are wild tigers in India. But is *their* ferocity and brutality to be the standard and pattern of *our* humanity? And because *they* have no compassion, are *we* to have no compassion? Because *they* have little or no reason, are *we* to have no reason? Or are *we* to become as very brutes as *they*? However, we need not go as far as India; for even in England dogs will worry and cocks will fight (though not so often, if we did not set them on, and prepare them for the battle). Yet what is that to us? Are we dogs? are we fighting cocks? are they to be our tutors and instructors, that we appeal to them for arguments to justify and palliate our inhumanity? No. Let tigers roar, let dogs worry, and cocks fight; but it is astonishing that *men*, who boast so much of the dignity of their nature, the superior excellence of their understanding, and the immortality of their souls (which, by-the-by, is a circumstance which cruel men above all others have the least reason to glory in), should disgrace their dignity and understanding by recurring to the practice of the low and confessedly *irrational* part of the creation in vindication of their own conduct."

The bulk of the book is occupied with references to scriptural texts on the duty of humaneness. The concluding moral is as follows: " See that no brute of any kind, whether intrusted to thy care, or coming in thy way, suffer through thy neglect or abuse. Let no views of profit, no compliance with custom, and no fear of the ridicule of the world, ever tempt thee to the least act of cruelty or injustice to any creature whatsoever. But let this be your invariable rule, everywhere, and at all times, to *do unto others as, in their condition, you would be done unto.*"

Disquisitions on Several Subjects. By Soame Jenyns. 1782.

Soame Jenyns (1704-1787) was an essayist, poet, and politician, whose writings, though now nearly forgotten, were highly estimated by his own generation. Chapter II. of his " Disquisitions " treats of " Cruelty to Inferior Animals," and is one of the best of the early treatises on the subject.

" No small part of mankind," he says, " derive their chief amusements from the death and sufferings of inferior animals ; a much greater consider them only as engines of wood or iron, useful in their several occupations. The carman drives his horse, and the carpenter his nail, by repeated blows ; and so long as these produce the desired effect, and they both go, they neither reflect nor care whether either of them have any sense of feeling. The butcher knocks down the stately ox with no more compassion than the blacksmith hammers a horse-shoe, and plunges his knife into the throat of the innocent lamb with as little reluctance as the tailor sticks his needle into the collar of a coat.

"If there are some few who, formed in a softer mould, view with pity the sufferings of these defenceless creatures, there is scarce one who entertains the least idea that justice or gratitude can be due to their merits or their services. The social and friendly dog is hanged without remorse, if by barking in defence of his master's person and property, he happens unknowingly to disturb his rest ; the generous horse, who has carried his ungrateful master for many years with ease and safety, worn out with age and infirmities contracted in his service, is by him condemned to end his miserable days in a dust-cart . . . . These, with innumerable other acts of cruelty, injustice, and ingratitude, are every day committed, not only with impunity, but without censure, and even without observation, but we may be assured that they cannot finally pass away unnoticed and unretaliated."

Introduction to the Principles of Morals and Legislation. By Jeremy Bentham. London, 1789 (printed 1780).

The following is the most notable passage in Bentham's works on the subject of animals' rights. It occurs in the chapter on "Limits between Private Ethics and the Art of Legislation," in which he shows that ethics concern a man's own conduct, legislation his treatment of others.

"What other agents, then, [*i.e.*, apart from oneself] are there, which, at the same time that they are under the influence of man's direction, are susceptible of happiness? They are of two sorts:

" I. Other human beings, who are styled *persons*.

" II. Other animals, which on account of their interests having been neglected by the insensibility of the ancient jurists, stand degraded into the class of *things*."

To the above is subjoined in a foot-note: "Under the Gentoo and Mahometan religions, the interests of the rest of the animal creation seem to have met with some attention. Why have they not, universally, with as much as those of human creatures, allowance made for the difference in point of sensibility? Because the Laws that are, have been the work of mutual fear—a sentiment which the less rational animals have not had the same means as man has of turning to account. Why *ought* they not? No reason can be given. If

Appendix

the being eaten were all, there is a very good reason why we should be suffered to eat such of them as we like to eat: we are the better for it, and they are never the worse . . . . If the being killed were all, there is very good reason why we should be suffered to kill such as molest us: we should be the worse for their living, and they are never the worse of being dead. But is there any reason why we should be suffered to torment them? Not any that I can see. Are there any why we should *not* be suffered to torment them? Yes, several. The day has been, I grieve to say in many places it is not yet past, in which the greater part of the species, under the denomination of *slaves*, have been treated by the law exactly upon the same footing as, in England, for example, the inferior races of animals are still. The day *may* come when the rest of the animal creation may acquire those rights which never could have been withholden from them but by the hand of tyranny. The French have already discovered that the blackness of the skin is no reason why a human being should be abandoned, without redress, to the caprice of a tormentor. It may come one day to be recognized that the number of the legs, the villosity of the skin, or the termination of the *os sacrum*, are reasons equally insufficient for abandoning a sensitive being to the same fate. What else is it should trace the insuperable line? Is it the faculty of reason, or, perhaps, the faculty of discourse? But a full-grown horse or dog is, beyond comparison, a more rational, as well as more conversable animal than an infant of a day, a week, or even a month old. But suppose the case were otherwise, what would it avail? The question is not, Can they *reason?* nor, Can they *talk?* but, Can they *suffer?*"

The Cry of Nature, or An Appeal to Mercy and Justice on behalf of the Persecuted Animals. By John Oswald. 1791.

John Oswald (1730-1793) was a native of Edinburgh, who served as an officer in India, and became intimately acquainted with Hindoo customs. He was a vegetarian, and the main object of his "Cry of Nature" is to advocate the discontinuance of flesh-eating. Much of what he writes on the animal question is eloquent and forcible, though the book is disfigured by an ornate and affected style. Here is an example :

"Sovereign despot of the world, lord of the life and death of every creature,—man, with the slaves of his tyranny, disclaims the ties of kindred. Howe'er attuned to the feelings of the human heart, their affections are the mere result of mechanic impulse; howe'er they may verge on human wisdom, their actions have only the semblance of sagacity : enlightened by the ray of reason, man is immensely removed from animals who have only instinct for their guide, and born to immortality, he scorns with the brutes that perish a social bond to acknowledge. Such are the unfeeling dogmas, which, early instilled into the mind, induce a callous insensibility, foreign to the native texture of the heart; such the cruel speculations which prepare us for the practice of that remorseless tyranny, and which palliate the foul oppression that, over inferior but fellow creatures, we delight to exercise."

A Vindication of the Rights of Brutes. London, 1792.

This little volume is attributed to Thomas Taylor, the Platonist, the translator of Porphyry's famous work on "Abstinence from the flesh of Living Beings." It was, as already stated, designed to throw ridicule on the theory of human rights.

In Chapter I. he ironically lays down the proposition "that God hath made all things equal." "It appears at first sight," he says, "somewhat singular that a moral truth of the highest importance and most illustrious evidence, should have been utterly unknown to the ancients, and not yet fully perceived, and universally acknowledged, even in such an enlightened age as the present. The truth I allude to is *the equality of all things, with respect to their intrinsic and real dignity and worth* . . . . I perceive, however, with no small delight that this sublime doctrine is daily gaining ground among the thinking part of mankind. Mr. Payne has already convinced thousands of the equality of men to each other;

and Mrs. Wollstonecraft has indisputably proved that women are in every respect naturally equal to men, not only in mental abilities, but likewise in bodily strength, boldness, and the like."

A Philosophical Treatise on Horses, and on the Moral Duties of Man towards the Brute Creation. By John Lawrence. Two vols. London, 1796-1798. Vol. I. chapter iii. deals with "The Rights of Beasts;" Vol. II. chapter i. with "The Philosophy of Sports."

John Lawrence, described as "a literary farmer," was an authority on agriculture and the management of domestic animals. He was a humanitarian, and was consulted by Richard Martin, M.P., on the details of the Ill-treatment of Cattle Bill, which became law in 1822. Humanity is the most conspicuous feature of Lawrence's writings. "From my first contributions to the periodical press," so he subsequently wrote, "I have embraced as many opportunities as were in my power of introducing the subject, and have never written any book on the care and management of animals wherein that important branch has been neglected."

"It has ever been," says Lawrence, "and still is, the invariable custom of the bulk of mankind, not even excepting legislators, both religious and civil, to look upon brutes as mere machines; animated, yet without souls; endowed with feelings, but utterly devoid of rights ; and placed without the pale of justice. From these defects, and from the idea, ill understood, of their being created merely for the use and purposes of man, have the feelings of beasts, their lawful, that is, natural interests and welfare, been sacrificed to his convenience, his cruelty, or his caprice.

" It is but too easy to demonstrate, by a series of melancholy facts, that brute creatures are not yet, in the contemplation of any people, reckoned within the scheme of general justice; that they reap only the benefit of a partial and inefficacious kind of compassion. Yet it is easy to prove, by analogies drawn from our own, that they also have souls; and perfectly consistent with reason to infer a gradation of intellect, from the spark which animates the most minute mortal exiguity, up to the sum of infinite intelligence, or the general soul of the universe. By a recurrence to principles, it will appear that life, intelligence, and feeling, necessarily imply rights. Justice, in which are included mercy, or compassion, obviously refer to sense and feeling. Now is the essence of justice divisible? Can there be one kind of justice for men, and another for brutes? Or is feeling in them a different thing to what it is in ourselves? Is not a beast produced by the same rule, and in the same order of generation with ourselves? Is not his body nourished by the same food, hurt by the same injuries ; his mind actuated by the same passions and affections which animate the human breast; and does not he also, at last, mingle his dust with ours, and in like manner surrender up the vital spark to the aggregate, or fountain of intelligence? Is this spark, or soul, to perish because it chanced to belong to a beast? Is it to become annihilate? Tell me, learned philosophers, how that may possibly happen."

On the Conduct of Man to Inferior Animals. By George Nicholson. Manchester, 1797.

The author of this work was a well-known Bradford printer (1760-1825), one of the pioneers of the cheap literature of the present day. In 1801 he published an enlarged edition, under the title of " The Primeval Diet of Man ; Arguments in favour of Vegetable Food ; On Man's Conduct to Animals, etc., etc." The book is in great measure a compilation of passages illustrative of man's cruelty to the lower kinds.

"In our conduct to animals," he writes in the "concluding reflections," "one plain rule may determine what form it ought to take, and prove an effectual guard against an improper treatment of them ;—a rule universally admitted as the foundation of moral rectitude ; *treat the animal which is in your power, in such a manner as you would willingly be treated, were you such an animal.* From men of imperious temper, inflated by wealth, devoted to sensual gratifications, and influenced by fashion, no share of humanity can be expected. He who is capable of enslaving his own species, of treating the inferior ranks of them with contempt or austerity, and who can be unmoved by their misfortunes, is a man formed of the materials of a cannibal, and will exercise his temper on the lower orders of animal life with inflexible obduracy. No arguments of truth or justice can affect such a hardened mind. Even persons of more gentle natures, having long been initiated in corrupt habits, do not readily listen to sensations of feeling; or, if the principles of justice, mercy, and tenderness be admitted, such principles are merely theoretical, and influence not their conduct. . . . .

" But the truly independent and sympathizing mind will ever derive satisfaction from the prospect of well-being, and will not incline to stifle convictions arising from the genuine evidences of truth. Without fear or hesitation he will become proof against the sneers of unfeeling men, exhibit an uniform example of humanity, and impress on others additional arguments and motives. . . . . In the present diseased and ruined state of society, the prospect is far distant when the System of Benevolence is likely to be generally adopted. The hope of reformation then arises from the intelligent, less corrupted, and younger part of mankind; but the numbers are comparatively few who think for **themselves, and who are not infected by long estab-**

lished and pernicious customs. It is a pleasure to foster the idea of a golden age regained, when the thought of the butcher shall not mingle with the sight of our flocks and herds. May the benevolent system spread to every corner of the globe! May we learn to recognize and to respect, in other animals, the feelings which vibrate in *ourselves!*"

An Essay on Humanity to Animals. By Thomas Young, Fellow of Trinity College, Cambridge. London, 1798.

"In offering to the public a book on Humanity to Animals," writes the author of this little volume, "I am sensible that I lay myself open to no small portion of ridicule; independent of all the common dangers to which authors are exposed. To many, no doubt, the subject which I have chosen will appear whimsical and uninteresting, and the particulars into which it is about to lead me ludicrous and mean. From the reflecting, however, and the humane I shall hope for a different opinion; and of these the number, I trust, among my countrymen is by no means inconsiderable. The exertions which have been made to diminish the sufferings of the prisoner, and to better the condition of the poor, the flourishing state of charitable institutions; the interest excited in the nation by the struggles for the abolition of the slave-trade; the growing detestation of religious persecution—all these and other circumstances induce me to believe that we have not been retrograde in Humanity during the present century: and I feel the more inclination and encouragement to execute the task to which I have set myself, inasmuch as humanity to animals presents itself to my mind as having an important connection with humanity towards mankind."

The author bases his plea for animals' rights on the light of nature. "Animals are endued with a capability of perceiving pleasure and pain; and from the abundant provision which we perceive in the world for the gratification of their several senses, we must conclude that the Creator wills the happiness of these his creatures, and consequently that humanity towards them is agreeable to him, and cruelty the contrary. This, I take it, is the foundation of the rights of animals, as far as they can be traced independently of scripture; and is, even by itself, decisive on the subject, being the same sort of argument as that on which moralists found the Rights of Mankind, as deduced from the Light of Nature."

The book opens with a general essay on humanity and cruelty, and contains chapters on sport, the treatment of horses, cruelties connected with the table, etc. etc. It is quoted approvingly by Thomas Forster and later advocates of humanity.

The Hare or Hunting Incompatible with Humanity. Dublin, 1800.

A story, by an anonymous writer, purporting to be told by a Hare.

Zoophilos. By Henry Crowe. Buckingham, 1819.

Contains chapters on sport, methods of slaughter for food, vivisection, etc.

Moral Inquiries on the Situation of Man and of Brutes. By Lewis Gompertz. London, 1824.

Lewis Gompertz was an ardent humanitarian and a mechanical inventor of no little ingenuity, many of his inventions being designed to save animal suffering. He died in 1861. From 1826 to 1832 he was secretary of the Society for the Prevention of Cruelty; but being then compelled to withdraw, owing to religious differences, he founded the Animals' Friend Society, and a journal of the same name.

"It needs but little power of rhetoric," he says in his opening chapter, "to prove that it is highly culpable in man to torture the brute creation for amusement; but, strange it would seem! this self-evident principle is not only openly violated by men whose rank in life has denied them the benefit of good education or leisure for reflection, but also by those with whom neither expense nor trouble has been spared towards the formation of their intellectual powers, even in their most abstracted recesses, and who in other respects delight in the application of their abilities towards everything that is good and meritorious. It is to be lamented that even philosophers frequently forget themselves on this subject, and relate, with the greatest indifference, the numerous barbarous and merciless experiments they have performed on the suffering and innocent brutes, even on those who show affection for them; and then coldly make their observations and calculations on every different form in which the agony produced by them manifests itself. But this they do for the advancement of science ! and expect much praise for their meritorious exertions ; forgetting that science should be subservient to the welfare of man and other animals, and ought not to be pursued merely through emulation, nor even for the sensual gratification the mind derives from them, at the expense of justice, the destruction of the happiness of others, and the production of their misery—as pleasure and pain are the only things of importance. . . . Forbid it that we should give assent to such tenets as these, and that we should suffer for one moment our reason to be veiled by such delusions ! But, on the contrary, let us hold fast every idea, and cherish every glimmering of such kind of knowledge as that which shall enable us to distinguish between *right* and *wrong*, what is due to one individual, what to another."

A later volume, " Fragments in Defence of Animals," 1852, is a collection of articles contributed by the same author to the " Animals' Friend."

The Rights of Animals, and Man's Obligation to treat them with Humanity. By William H. Drummond, D. D. London, 1838.

A guarded essay, in which the writer pleads for the restriction of vivisection, but justifies flesh-eating and fieldsports.

Philozoia, or Moral Reflections on the actual condition of the Animal Kingdom, and the means of improving the same. By T. Forster. Brussels, 1839.

The author of this excellent treatise, which is addressed to Lewis Gompertz, was a distinguished naturalist and astronomer who had taken an active part in the founding of the Animals' Friend Society. He was born in 1789, and died at Brussels in 1860, having lived abroad during the latter part of his life. A section of his book is devoted to the "Condition of Animals on the Continent."

"One of the surest means," he says, "of bettering the condition of animals will be to improve the character of man, by giving to children a humane rational education, and, above all, setting before them examples of kindness. Hitherto nothing has been so much neglected as this duty, and the evil effects of this neglect have been generally visible in the character of the people. At present it is better understood; but a great deal remains to be done, and as the education of children will not be thoroughly reformed till their instructors are first set to rights, I should propose to your society to procure the delivery of lectures on the subject at the various mechanics' institutes in England."

Of sport, he says: "You will do well to reflect on this, and to inquire whether the just suppression of bull-baiting, cock-fighting, and other such vulgar and vicious pastimes, should not, as the age becomes more and more civilized, be followed by the abolition of fox-hunting, and all sporting not immediately directed to the object of obtaining game for food by the most easy and expeditious means."

On the subject of "the Cruelty connected with the Culinary Art," he has also some wise remarks: "Some persons in Europe carry their notions about cruelty to animals so far as not to allow themselves to eat animal food. Many very intelligent men have, at different times of their lives, abstained wholly from flesh; and this, too, with very considerable advantage to their health. . . . All these facts, taken collectively, point to a period in the progress of civilization when men will cease to slay their fellow-mortals in the animal world for food. . . . The return of this paradisical state may be rather remote ; but in the meantime we ought to make the experiment, and set an example of humanity by abstaining, if not from all, at least from those articles of cookery with which any particular cruelty may be connected, such as veal, when the calves are killed in the ordinary way."

Equally noteworthy are the chapters on "Cruelty in Surgical Experiments," and " Animals considered as our Fellow Creatures."

The Obligation and Extent of Humanity to Brutes, principally considered with reference to the Domesticated Animals. By W. Youatt. London, 1839.

William Youatt (1777-1847), Professor in the Royal Veterinary College, and author of many standard works on veterinary subjects, was a member of the Society for the Prevention of Cruelty.

"The claims of humanity," he says in his introduction, "however they may be neglected or outraged in a variety of respects, are recognized by every ethical writer. They are truly founded on reason and on scripture, and in fact are indelibly engraven on the human heart.

"But to what degree are they recognized and

obeyed? To what extent are they inculcated, not only in many excellent treatises on moral philosophy, but by the great majority of the expounders of the scriptures? We answer with shame, and with an astonishment that increases upon us in proportion as we think of the subject,—the duties of humanity are represented as extending to our fellow-men, to the victims of oppression or misfortune, the deaf and the dumb, the blind, the slave, the beggared prodigal, and even the convicted felon—all these receive more or less sympathy; but, with exceptions, few and far between, not a writer pleads for the innocent and serviceable creatures—*brutes* as they are termed—that minister to our wants, natural or artificial.

" Nevertheless, the claims of the lower animals to humane treatment, or at least to exemption from abuse, are as good as any that man can urge upon man. Although less intelligent, and not immortal, they are susceptible of pain: but because they cannot remonstrate, nor associate with their fellows in defence of their rights, our best theologians and philosophers have not condescended to plead their cause, or even to make mention of them; although, as just asserted, they have as much right to protection from ill-usage as the best of their masters have.

" Nay, the matter has been carried further than this. At no very distant period, the right of wantonly torturing the inferior animals, as caprice or passion dictated, was unblushingly claimed; and it was asserted that the prevention of this was an interference with the rights and liberties of man ! Strange that at the beginning of the nineteenth century this should have been the avowed opinion of some of the British legislators ; and that the advocate of the claims of the brute should have been regarded as a fool or a madman, or a compound of both."

The book contains chapters on the usefulness and good qualities of the inferior animals, the application of the principle of humanity, the dissection of living animals, the study of natural history, etc.

"The Morality of Field Sports." By Professor E. A. Freeman, *Fortnightly Review*, October, 1869.

This article, together with a reply by Anthony Trollope and a rejoinder by Prof. Freeman, was reprinted (1900) under the title of *The Morality of Hunting*, by Mr. R. K. Gaye, of Trinity College, Cambridge.

A Few Notes on Cruelty to Animals. By Ralph Fletcher. London, 1846.

This treatise, by a medical man, President of the Gloucester S.P.C.A., deals with various forms of cruelty to the domestic animals. I quote a passage from the Introductory Note :—

Appendix

"The quantity and variety of suffering endured by the lower creation of animals when domesticated by man have struck the author with awful force, but more especially since his connection with a Society for their alleviation: a mingled feeling of pity, horror, and anxiety is left on the mind at the helpless and certain fate of such a vast crowd of innocent beings . . . There is a moral as well as a physical character to all animal life, however humble it may be,—enveloped indeed in obscurity, and with a mysterious solemnity which must ever belong to the secrets of the Eternal. Let us then approach with caution the unknown character of the brute, as being an emanation from Himself; and treat with tenderness and respect the helpless creatures derived from such a source. . . .

"Let us not, therefore, enter into the needless question whether animals have souls. We behold the miseries of the poor dumb creature, we feel that we have free-will sufficient, and the means, to lighten his burdens; let us therefore commence with energy this really benevolent purpose, rather than assume theories of his happiness which are but apologies for our want of feeling, our avarice, or our indolence."

Some Talk about Animals and their Masters. By Sir Arthur Helps. London, 1873.

This pleasant and popular little book contains many good remarks about animals. But there is no attempt in it to advance any distinct or consistent view of the question.

Man and Beast, here and hereafter. By the Rev. J. G. Wood. London, 1874.

This is a plea for animal immortality, by a well-known naturalist. His plan is threefold. First, to show that the Bible does not deny a future life to animals. Secondly, to prove by anecdotes, "that the lower animals share with man the attributes of Reason, Language, Memory, a sense of moral responsibility, Unselfishness, and Love, all of which belong to the spirit and not to the body." Thirdly, to conclude that, as man expects to retain these qualities after death, the presumption is in favour of the animals also retaining them.

A list of numerous works on the subject of animal immortality may be found in "The Literature of the Doctrine of a Future Life," Appendix II., New York, 1871, by Ezra Abbot.

The Rights of an Animal, a new Essay in Ethics. By Edward Byron Nicholson, M.A. London, 1879.

This plea for animals' rights gives much interesting information on the animal question in general. It contains a reprint of part of John Lawrence's chapter on "'The Rights of Beasts," with a memoir of the author.

Appendix

A Plea for Mercy to Animals. By J. Macaulay. London, 1881.

The author directs his argument, on religious grounds, against vivisection and the deliberate ill-usage of animals; but does not advocate any distinct theory of rights.

The Ethics of Diet, a Catena of Authorities deprecatory of the habit of Flesh-eating. By Howard Williams, M.A. London and Manchester, 1883.

Of all recent books on the subject of animals' rights this is by far the most scholarly and exhaustive. Though written primarily from a vegetarian standpoint, it contains a vast amount of general information on the various phases of the animal question, and is therefore invaluable to any earnest student of that subject. The key-note of the book is struck in the following passage of the preface:

" In the general constitution of life on our globe, suffering and slaughter, it is objected, are the normal and constant condition of things—the strong relentlessly and cruelly preying upon the weak in endless succession—and, it is asked, why then should the human species form an exception to the general rule, and hopelessly fight against Nature? To this it is to be replied, first: that, although too certainly an unceasing and cruel internecine warfare has been waged upon this atomic globe of ours from the first origin of Life until now, yet, apparently, there has been going on a slow, but not uncertain, progress towards the ultimate elimination of the crueller phenomena of Life; that, if the carnivora form a very large proportion of living beings, yet the non-carnivora are in the majority; and lastly, what is still more to the purpose, that Man most evidently by his origin and physical organization belongs not to the former but to the latter; besides and beyond which, that in proportion as he boasts himself (and as he is seen at his best, and only so far, he boasts himself with justice) to be the highest of all the gradually ascending and co-ordinated series of living beings, so is he, in that proportion, bound to prove his right to the supreme place and power, and his asserted claims to moral as well as mental superiority, by his conduct. In brief, in so far only as he proves himself to be the beneficent ruler and pacificator—and not the selfish tyrant—of the world, can he have any just title to the moral pre-eminence."

Our Duty towards Animals. By Philip Austin. London, 1885.

The author of this pamphlet, discussing the question "in the light of Christian philosophy," argues that animals have no rights, and quotes many passages to prove that such a theory is contrary to the teaching of Scripture and the early Fathers. "The morality," he says, "which satisfied S.

Appendix

Augustine may surely be considered good enough for the English churchman of to-day." He ridicules Sir A. Helps' idea of showing "courtesy" to animals. "It should be remembered that they are our slaves, not our equals, and for this reason it is well to keep up such practices as hunting and fishing, driving and riding, merely to demonstrate in a practical way man's dominion over the brutes. . . . It is found that an advocacy of the rights of brutes is associated with the lowest phases of morality, and that kindness to the brutes is a mere work of supererogation."

This essay is well worth the attention of humanitarians, as coming from an out-spoken opponent of animals' rights,—one whose views are an interesting survival of the mediæval spirit of utter indifference to animal suffering. It sets forth and applauds with singular frankness—I had almost said brutality— the disregard which the Catholic Church has always shown for "the beasts that perish;" thereby affording a valuable object-lesson as to the only logical alternative to the creed of humanity. That Mr. Austin's argument is not a burlesque, but a fair exposition of Catholic doctrine, may be shown by the following significant passage from an article on "The Lower Animals" in the "Catholic Dictionary," by W. E. Addis and T. Arnold, 1884.

"As the lower animals have no duties, since they are destitute of free will, without which the performance of duty is impossible, so they have no rights, for right and duty are correlative terms. The brutes are made for man, who has the same right over them which he has over plants and stones. He may, according to the express permission of God, given to Noe, kill them for his food; and if it is lawful to destroy them for food, and this without strict necessity, it must also be lawful to put them to death, or to inflict pain on them, for any good and reasonable end, such as the promotion of man's knowledge, health, etc., or even for the purposes of recreation. But a limitation must be introduced here. It is never lawful for a man to take pleasure directly in the pain given to brutes, because, in doing so, man degrades and brutalizes his own nature."

The Duties and the Rights of Man. By J. B. Austin, 1887.

In Book V. the author deals with the "Indirect Duties of Man towards Animals." While not allowing more than "instinct" to animals, and asserting that "in the whole of the animal kingdom there is not a single specimen possessing even a spark of reason," he advocates humaneness on the ground that animals are "sensitive beings." "By cultivating the faculty of sympathy, and by considering that sensibility to pain is common to both men and animals, we soon perceive that to inflict needless and unjust pain upon the latter, is to sin against one's own nature, and therefore to commit a crime."

Appendix

Animals' Rights, considered in relation to Social Progress. By Henry S. Salt. London, 1892.

Moral Philosophy. By Joseph Rickaby, S. J. London, 1892.

Contains a statement of the Catholic position in denial of rights to animals.

Natural Rights. By David G. Ritchie. London, 1895.

See page 133 of this book

The New Charter, a discussion of the Rights of Men and the Rights of Animals.

Essays published by the Humanitarian League. London, 1896.

Evolutional Ethics and Animal Psychology. By E. P. Evans. London, 1898.

The Nature and Development of Animal Intelligence. By Wesley Mills, M.D. London, 1898.

Kith and Kin: Poems of Animal Life. Edited by Henry S. Salt. London, 1901.

Every Living Creature. By Ralph Waldo Trine. London, 1901.

The Basis of Morality. By Arthur Schopenhauer. Translated by A. B. Bullock. London, 1903.

The Universal Kinship. By J. Howard Moore. London, 1906.

This brilliantly written work asserts the scientific basis of humanitarianism, and treats of the subject of animals' rights under three heads—the physical, the psychical, and the ethical kinship between human and subhuman.

The New Ethics. By J. Howard Moore. London, 1907.

The Church and Kindness to Animals. London, 1907.

A translation from the French, *L'Église et la Pitié envers les Animaux* (1903), in vindication of the Catholic Church against the charge of indifference to animal suffering.

The Place of Animals in Human Thought. By the Countess Martinengo Cesaresco. London, 1909.

A work of value to those who are studying the psychological aspect of the question.

The Mahatma and the Hare. By H. Rider Haggard. London, 1911

Killing for Sport. By various writers, edited by Henry S. Salt, with Introduction by G. Bernard Shaw. London, 1915.

The Publications of the Humanitarian League. Pamphlets on various subjects, 1891-1919.

Suffering and Wrong: The Message of the New Religion. By Francis Wood. London, 1916.

Savage Survivals. By J. Howard Moore. London, 1916.

The Great Kinship. An Anthology of Humanitarian Poetry, edited by Bertram Lloyd. London, 1921.

The Soul of an Animal. By T. S. Hawkins, London, 1921.

AN UPDATED BIBLIOGRAPHY

Prepared by

CHARLES R. MAGEL*
MOORHEAD STATE UNIVERSITY
MOORHEAD, MINNESOTA

BOOKS

Adams, Richard, *The Plague Dogs*, Alfred A. Knopf, New York, 1978. (A novel about two dogs who escape from an experimental laboratory; inspired, in part, by Peter Singer's *Animal Liberation*.)

Adams, Richard, *Watership Down*, Macmillan Publishing Co., New York, 1972. (A novel. The reader enters the rabbit world, seeing things through rabbits' eyes, smelling the scents as only animals living in the wild can, living their terrors and triumphs.)

Agius, Dom Ambrose, *God's Animals*, Catholic Study Circle for Animal Welfare, 39 Onslow Gardens, London E. 18, 1970.

* I would like to express my appreciation to Tom Regan (North Carolina State University) and Peter Singer (Monash University) for a number of very helpful suggestions.

Appendix

Altman, Nathaniel, *Eating for Life*, Theosophical Publishing House, Wheaton, Illinois, 1977. (On vegetarianism.)

Amaral, Anthony A., *Movie Horses: Their Treatment and Training*, The Bobbs-Merrill Co., Indianapolis, Indiana, 1967.

Amory, Cleveland, *Man Kind? Our Incredible War on Wildlife*, Harper & Row, New York, 1974.

Animal Expressions, 1967, Animal Welfare Institute, Washington, D.C. (A photographic footnote to Charles Darwin's *Expression of the Emotions in Man and Animals*.)

Batten, Peter, *Living Trophies: A Shocking Look at the Conditions in America's Zoos*, Thomas Y. Crowell, Co., New York, 1976.

Bayly, M. Beddow, *The Futility of Experiments on Animals*, National Anti-Vivisection Society, London, 1954.

Bayly, M. Beddow, *More Spotlights on Vivisection*, National Anti-Vivisection Society, London, 1960.

Bayly, M. Beddow, *Spotlights on Vivisection*, National Anti-Vivisection Society, London, 1946.

Bennett, Jonathan F., *Rationality*, Humanities Press, New York, 1964. (Includes an analysis of the behavior of honey bees and other animals, in relation to language, intelligence and rationality.)

Blake, Henry N., *Talking with Horses*, E. P. Dutton & Co., New York, 1975.

Boas, George, *The Happy Beast in French Thought of the Seventeenth Century*, Octagon Books, New York, 1966. (The views of Montaigne, Descartes and other French writers on animals.)

Brophy, Brigid, *Hackenfeller's Ape*, Penguin, London, 1968. (A novel about a scientist who saves an ape from being sent up in a rocket.)

Carson, Gerald, *Men, Beasts, and Gods: A History of Cruelty and Kindness to Animals*, Charles Scribner's Sons, New York, 1972.

Clark, Stephen R. L., *The Moral Status of Animals*, Oxford University Press, New York, 1977.

Clarke, Francis E., ed., *Poetry's Plea for Animals: An Anthology of Justice and Mercy for Our Kindred in Fur and Feathers*, Lothrop, Lee and Shepard Co., Boston, 1927.

Cohen, Noah J., *The Concept of Tsa'ar Ba'ale Hayyim (Kindness, and the Prevention of Cruelty to Animals): Its Bases and Development in Biblical, Midrashic and Talmudic Literature*, Catholic University of America, Washington, D.C., 1953.

Curtis, Patricia, *Animal Rights*, Four Winds Press, New York, 1980.

Darwin, Charles, *The Expression of the Emotions in Man and Animals*, Philosophical Library, New York, 1955.

DeLevie, Dagobert, *The Modern Idea of the Prevention of Cruelty to Animals and Its Reflection in English Poetry*, S. F. Vanni, New York, 1947.

Appendix

Derby, Pat, *The Lady and Her Tiger*, E. P. Dutton & Co., New York, 1976. (About animal training for circuses and other entertainment.)

Dewar, James. *The Rape of Noah's Ark*, William Kimber, London, 1969.

Diner, Jeff, *Physical and Mental Suffering of Experimental Animals*, A Review of Scientific Literature: 1975-1978. Animal Welfare Institute, Washington, D.C., 1978.

Duffy, Maureen, *I Want to Go to Moscow*, Hodder, London, 1973. (A novel about a band of radicals who blow up things to save animals.)

The Ethology and Ethics of Farm Animal Production, Proceedings of the 28th Annual Meeting, Commission on Animal Management and Health, Brussels, Belgium, August, 1977. Birkhauser Verlag, P. O. Box 34, CH-4010, Basel, Switzerland.

Evans, Edward, *The Criminal Prosecution and Capital Punishment of Animals*, William Heinemann, London, 1906.

Field-Fisher, Thomas G., *Animals and the Law*, Universities Federation for Animal Welfare, London, 1964.

Fox, Michael W., *Between Animal and Man*, Coward, McCann & Geoghegan, New York, 1976.

Fox, Michael W., *Towards the New Eden: Animal Rights and Human Liberation*, Viking, New York, 1979.

French, Richard D., *Antivivisection and Medical Science in Victorian Society*, Princeton University Press, Princeton, New Jersey, 1975.

Frey, R. G., *Interests and Rights: The Case Against Animals*, Clarendon Press, Oxford, forthcoming.

Gelli, Giovanni Battista, *Circe*, trans. by Thomas Brown and Robert Adam, Cornell University Press, Ithaca, New York, 1963. (Consisting of ten dialogues between Ulysses and several men transformed into beasts, satirically representing the various passions of mankind and the many infelicities of human life.)

Giehl, Dudley, *Vegetarianism: A Way of Life*, with a Foreword by Isaac Bashevis Singer, Harper & Row, New York, 1979.

Godlovitch, Stanley and Roslind, and Harris, John, eds., *Animals, Men and Morals*, Gollancz, London, 1971; and Taplinger, New York, 1971.

Griffin, Donald R., *The Question of Animal Awareness*, Rockefeller University Press, New York, 1976.

Harrison, Ruth, *Animal Machines: The New Factory Farming Industry*, V. Stuart, London, 1964.

Harwood, Dix, *Love for Animals and How It Developed in Great Britain*, Columbia University Dissertation, New York, 1928.

Hastings, Hester, *Man and Beast in French Thought of the Eighteenth Century*, The Johns Hopkins Studies in Romance Literatures and Languages, Vol. XXVII, Johns Hopkins Press, Baltimore, Maryland, 1936.

Hediger, Heini, *Man and Animal in the Zoo*, trans. by Gwynne Vevers and Winwood Reade, Delacorte Press, New York, 1969.

Hediger, Heini, *Wild Animals in Captivity*, trans. by G. Sircom, Dover, New York, 1950.

Hendrick, George, *Henry Salt: Humanitarian, Reformer, and Man of Letters*, University of Illinois Press, Urbana, Illinois, 1977.

Holmes-Gore, Vincent A., *These We Have Not Loved*, C. W. Daniel Co., Ashingdon, Rochford, Essex, England, 1971. (Christian attitude toward animals.)

Hume, Charles W., *Man and Beast*, Universities Federation for Animal Welfare, London, 1962.

Hume, Charles W., *The Status of Animals in the Christian Religion*, Universities Federation for Animal Welfare, London, 1957.

Hutchings, Monica M., and Caver, Mavis, *Man's Dominion: Our Violation of the Animal World*, Rupert Hart-Davis, London, 1970. (Performing animals, bull fighting, rodeos, pets, zoos, animal traffic, hunting, factory farming, furs, experimenting on animals.)

Johnson, Edward, *Species and Morality*, Doctoral Dissertation, Princeton University, 1976. Available from University International Dissertation Copies, Ann Arbor, Michigan, Order No. 77-2150, 258 pp.

Keele, C. A., and Smith, R., eds., *The Assessment of Pain in Men and Animals*, Universities Federation for Animal Welfare, London, 1962.

Kellert, Stephen R., *Policy Implications of a National Study of American Attitudes and Behavioral Relations to Animals*, September, 1978. For sale by Superintendent of Documents, U. S. Government Printing Office, Washington, D.C., Stock Number 024-010-00482-7. (Working papers presented to the U. S. Fish and Wildlife Service. Considers attitudes and behavioral relations of hunters, anti-hunters, various social demographic groups, backpackers, birdwatchers, zoo enthusiasts, trappers, financial contributors to animal welfare causes, animal raisers, pet owners, rodeo enthusiasts.)

Klaits, Joseph and Barrie, eds., *Animals and Man in Historical Perspective*, Harper & Row, New York, 1974.

Kotzwinkle, William, *Doctor Rat*, Alfred A. Knopf, New York, 1976. (A novel about a rat in a laboratory.)

Lappé, Frances M., *Diet for a Small Planet*, Ballantine Books, New York, 1971.

Linzey, Andrew, *Animal Rights: A Christian Assessment of Man's Treatment of Animals*, SCM Press, London, 1976.

Martin, Ernest W., *The Case against Hunting*, Dennis Dobson, London, 1959.

Martinengo-Cesaresco, Evelyn L. H., *The Place of Animals in Human Thought*, T. F. Unwin, London, 1909. (There is a copy of this book in the University of Minnesota Library.)

Mason, Jim, and Singer, Peter, *Animal Factories*, Crown, New York, 1980.

Midgley, Mary, *Beast and Man: The Roots of Human Nature*, Cornell University Press, Ithaca, New York, 1978.

Mill, John Stuart, *Utilitarianism*, The Bobbs-Merrill Co., Indianapolis, Indiana, 1957.

Moore, Patrick, ed., *Against Hunting*, Gollancz, London, 1965.

The Moral Scientific and Economic Aspects of Research Techniques Not Involving the Use of Living Animals, National Anti-Vivisection Society, London, 1977. (Text of speeches given at Brighton Conference, March, 1976.)

Morris, Richard Knowles, and Fox, Michael W., eds., *On the Fifth Day: Animal Rights and Human Ethics*, Acropolis Press, Washington, D.C., 1978.

Morse, Mel, *Ordeal of the Animals*, Prentice-Hall, Englewood Cliffs, New Jersey, 1968.

Porphyry, *On Abstinence from Animal Food*, trans. by T. Taylor, ed. by Esmé Wynne-Tyson, Centaur Press, London, 1965.

Pratt, Dallas, *Painful Experiments on Animals—And the Alternatives*, Argus Archives, New York, forthcoming.

Regan, Tom, ed., *Matters of Life and Death*, Random House, New York, 1979.

Regan, Tom, and Singer, Peter, eds., *Animal Rights and Human Obligations*, Prentice-Hall, Englewood Cliffs, New Jersey, 1976.

Regenstein, Lewis, *The Politics of Extinction*, Macmillan Publishing Co., New York, 1975.

Report of the Technical Committee to Enquire

into the *Welfare of Animals Kept under Intensive Livestock Husbandry Systems* ("The Brambell Report"), Command Paper 2836, Her Majesty's Stationery Office, London, 1965.

Rosenfield, Leonora, *From Beast-Machine to Man-Machine: The Theme of Animal Soul in French Letters from Descartes to La Mettrie*, Octagon Books, New York, 1968.

Ruesch, Hans, *Slaughter of the Innocent*, Bantam, New York, 1978. (A history and critique of animal experimentation in the medical and drug industries, with the thesis that such experimentation is doing more harm—to humans—than good.)

Ryder, Richard, *Victims of Science*, Davis-Poynter, London, 1975.

Ryder, Richard, and Paterson, David, eds., *Animals' Rights: A Symposium*, Centaur Press, London, 1979.

St. John-Stevas, Norman, *The Right to Life*, Holt, Rinehart & Winston, New York, 1964.

Salt, Henry S., *The Humanities of Diet*, The Vegetarian Society, Manchester, 1914.

Salt, Henry S., *The Logic of Vegetarianism*, London Vegetarian Society, London, 1933.

Salt, Henry S., *Seventy Years Among Savages*, G. Allen & Unwin, London, 1921; also Thomas Seltzer, New York, 1921.

Salt, Henry S., ed. *Cruelties of Civilization*, Humanitarian League Publications, Vol.2, William Reeves, London. (There is a copy of this book in Princeton University Library.)

Appendix

Scheffer, Victor B., *A Voice for Wildlife*, Charles Scribner's Sons, New York, 1974. (Hunting, killing for subsistence, killing for the fur trade, killing for science, sealing, an ethic toward wildlife, etc.)

Schweitzer, Albert, *The Animal World of Albert Schweitzer*, trans. and ed. by Charles R. Joy, Beacon Press, Boston, 1950.

Schweitzer, Albert, *The Teaching of Reverence for Life*, Holt, Rinehart & Winston, New York. 1965.

Shaw, George Bernard, *Shaw on Vivisection*, ed. by G.H. Bowker, George Allen & Unwin, London, 1949; also Alethea Publications, Chicago, 1950.

Singer, Peter, *Animal Liberation, A New Ethics for Our Treatment of Animals*, A New York Review Book distributed by Random House, New York, 1975; also Avon Books, New York, 1977.

Singer, Peter, *Practical Ethics*, Cambridge University Press, Cambridge, 1979. (Chapters 3–5 are relevant to the animal issue.)

Stewart, Jean, *Traps and Trapping, Furs and Fashion*, Argus Archives, New York, 1977.

Stone, Christopher D., *Should Trees Have Standing? Toward Legal Rights for Natural Objects*, Kaufmann, Los Altos, California, 1974.

Sussman, Vic, *The Vegetarian Alternative*, Rodale Press, Emmaus, Pennsylvania, 1978.

Turner, Ernest S., *All Heaven in a Rage*, Michael Joseph, London, 1964.

Tuttle, Margaret W., *The Crimson Cage*, Tashmoo Press, Martha's Vineyard, Mass., 1978. (Fiction:

based on facts about pounds, dealers, vivisection.)

Visscher, Maurice B., *Ethical Constraints and Imperatives in Medical Research*, Thomas, Springfield, Illinois, 1975.

Vyvyan, John, *The Dark Face of Science*, Michael Joseph, London, 1971. Also Transatlantic Arts, Levittown, New York, 1972.

Vyvyan, John, *In Pity and in Anger: A Study of the Use of Animals in Science*, Michael Joseph, London, 1969.

Westacott, Evalyn A., *A Century of Vivisection and Anti-Vivisection*, C. W. Daniel Co., Ashingdon, Rochford, Essex, England, 1949.

Westacott, Evalyn A., *Boomerang*, Battley Bros., London, 1950. (Some considerations against vivisection.)

Westacott, Evalyn, comp., *Spotlight on Performing Animals*, Rochford (Ex.), C. W. Daniel Co., Ashingdon, Rochford, Essex, England, 1962. (Extracts from evidence given before the Select Committee of 1921 and 1922.)

White, Terence H., trans. and ed., *The Book of Beasts*, Cape, London, 1956. (A translation from a Latin bestiary of the twelfth century. See especially pp. 230–270.)

Winsten, Stephen, *Salt and His Circle*, Hutchinson & Co., London, 1951.

Wynne-Tyson, Esmé, *The Philosophy of Compassion*, V. Stuart, London, 1962.

Wynne-Tyson, Jon, *The Civilized Alternative*,

Beekman Publishers, Brooklyn Heights, New York, 1972.

Wynne-Tyson, Jon, *Food for a Future; The Ecological Priority of a Humane Diet*, Davis-Poynter, London, 1975.

PHILOSOPHICAL JOURNAL ARTICLES

Auxter, Thomas, "The Right Not to Be Eaten," *Inquiry*, Vol. 22, Spring-Summer, 1979.

Becker, Earnest, "Toward the Merger of Animal and Human Studies," *Philosophy of the Social Sciences*, Vol. 4, June-September, 1974.

Benson, John, "Duty and the Beast," *Philosophy*, Vol. 53, October, 1978.

Broadie, Alexander, and Pybus, Elizabeth, "Kant's Treatment of Animals," *Philosophy*, Vol. 49, October, 1974.

Burch, Robert W., "Animals, Rights and Claims," *Southwestern Journal of Philosophy*, Vol. 8, Summer, 1977.

Clark, Stephen R. L., "Animal Wrongs," *Analysis*, Vol. 38, No. 3, June, 1978.

Clark, Stephen R. L., "The Rights of Wild Things," *Inquiry*, Vol. 22, Spring-Summer, 1979.

Collins, A. W., "How Could One Tell Were a Bee to Guide His Behavior by a Rule?" *Mind*, Vol. 77, October, 1968.

Cottingham, John, " 'A Brute to the Brutes?': Descartes' Treatment of Animals," *Philosophy*, Vol. 53, October, 1978.

Davis, William H., "Man-Eating Aliens," *Journal of Value Inquiry*, Vol. 10, Fall, 1976.

Devine, Philip E., "The Moral Basis of Vegetarianism," *Philosophy*, Vol. 53, October, 1978.

Diamond, Cora, "Eating Meat and Eating People," *Philosophy*, Vol. 53, October, 1978.

Donaghy, Kevin, "Singer on Speciesism," *Philosophic Exchange*, Vol. 1, Summer, 1974.

Elliot, Robert, "Regan on the Sorts of Beings That Can Have Rights," *Southern Journal of Philosophy*, Vol. 16, Spring, 1978.

Fowler, Corbin, "Freedom: Animal Rights, Human Rights, and Super-human Rights,"*Auslegung*, Vol. 4, 1976.

Fox, Michael A., " 'Animal Liberation': A Critique," *Ethics*, Vol. 88, January, 1978.

Fox, Michael A., "Animal Suffering and Rights," *Ethics*, Vol. 88, January, 1978.

Francis, Leslie Pickering, and Norman, Richard, "Some Animals Are More Equal than Others," *Philosophy*,Vol. 53, October, 1978.

Frey, R. G., "Animal Rights," *Analysis*, Vol. 37, June, 1977.

Frey, R. G., "Interests and Animal Rights," *Philosophical Quarterly*, Vol. 27, July, 1977.

Frey, R. G., "Rights, Interests, Desires and Beliefs," *American Philosophical Quarterly*, Vol. 16, No. 3, July, 1979.

Fuller, B. A. G., "The Messes Animals Make in Metaphysics," *The Journal of Philosophy*, Vol. 46, December, 1949.

Appendix

Godlovitch, Roslind, "Animals and Morals," *Philosophy*, Vol. 46, January, 1971.

Goodpaster, Kenneth, "On Being Morally Considerable," *Journal of Philosophy*, Vol. 75, June, 1978.

Goodrich, T., "The Morality of Killing," *Philosophy*, Vol. 44, April, 1969.

Grene, Marjorie, "People and Other Animals," *Philosophical Forum* (Boston), Vol. 3, Winter, 1972.

Hall, Elton A., and King-Farlow, John, "Man, Beast, and Philosophical Psychology," *The British Journal for the Philosophy of Science*, Vol. 16, August, 1965.

Hartshorne, Charles, "The Rights of the Subhuman World," *Environmental Ethics*, January, 1979.

Haworth, Lawrence, "Rights, Wrongs, and Animals," *Ethics*, Vol. 88, January, 1978.

Jamieson, Dale, and Regan, Tom, "Animal Rights: A Reply to Frey," *Analysis*, Vol. 38, January, 1978.

Jones, Hardy, "Reply: Concerning the Moral Status of Animals," *Southwestern Journal of Philosophy*, Vol. 8, Summer, 1977.

Lockwood, Michael, "Singer on Killing and the Preference for Life," *Inquiry*, Vol. 22, Spring-Summer, 1979.

Lowry, Jon, "Natural Rights: Men and Animals," *Southwestern Journal of Philosophy*, Vol. 6, Summer, 1975.

McCloskey, H. J., "Moral Rights and Animals,"

Inquiry, Vol. 22, Spring-Summer, 1979.

McCloskey, H. J., "The Right to Life," *Mind*, Vol. 84, July, 1975.

McCloskey, H. J., "Rights," *Philosophical Quarterly*, Vol. 15, April, 1965.

McGinn, Colin, "Evolution, Animals, and the Basis of Morality," *Inquiry*, Vol. 22, Spring-Summer, 1979.

MacIver, A. M., "Ethics and the Beetle," *Analysis*, Vol. 8, April, 1948. Also in *Ethics*, ed. by Judith J. Thomson and Gerald Dworkin, Harper & Row, New York, 1968.

Mackie, J. L., "Can There Be a Right-Based Moral Theory?" *Midwest Studies in Philosophy*, Vol. 3, 1978, pp. 350-359.

Malcolm, Norman, "Thoughtless Brutes," *Proceedings of American Philosophical Association*, Vol 46, 1972-73. Also in Malcolm, Norman, *Thought and Knowledge*, Cornell University Press, Ithaca, 1977.

Margolis, Joseph, "Animals Have No Rights and Are Not the Equal of Humans," *Philosophic Exchange*, Vol. 1, Summer, 1974.

Martin, Michael, "A Critique of Moral Vegetarianism," *Reason Papers*, Vol. 3, Fall, 1976.

Matthews, Gareth B., "Animals and the Unity of Psychology," *Philosophy*, Vol. 53, October, 1978.

Midgley, Mary, "The Concept of Beastliness: Philosophy, Ethics and Animal Behavior," *Philosophy*, Vol. 48, April, 1973.

Naess, Arne, "Self-realization in Mixed Communities of Humans, Bears, Sheep, and Wolves," *Inquiry*, Vol. 22, Spring-Summer, 1979.

Narveson, Jan, "Animal Rights," *Canadian Journal of Philosophy*, Vol. 7, March, 1977.

Passmore, John, "The Treatment of Animals," *Journal of History of Ideas*, Vol. 36, April-June, 1975.

Pybus, Elizabeth M. and Broadie, Alexander, "Kant and the Maltreatment of Animals," *Philosophy*, Vol. 53, October, 1978.

Pybus, Elizabeth and Broadie, Alexander, "Kant's Treatment of Animals," *Philosophy*, Vol. 49, October, 1974.

Reeve, E. Gavin, "Speciesism and Equality," *Philosophy*, Vol. 53, October, 1978.

Regan, Tom, "Animal Rights and Human Wrongs," *Etyka* (Poland), January, 1980.

Regan, Tom, "Broadie and Pybus on Kant," *Philosophy*, Vol. 51, October, 1976.

Regan, Tom, "Cruelty, Kindness and Unnecessary Suffering," *Philosophy*, forthcoming.

Regan, Tom, "An Examination and Defense of One Argument Concerning Animal Rights," *Inquiry*, Vol. 22, Spring-Summer, 1979.

Regan, Tom, "Feinberg on What Sorts of Beings Can Have Rights," *Southern Journal of Philosophy*, Vol. 14, Winter, 1976.

Regan, Tom, "Fox's Critique of Animal Liberation," *Ethics*, Vol. 88, January, 1978.

Regan, Tom, "Frey on Interests and Animal

Rights," *Philosophical Quarterly*, Vol. 27, October, 1977.

Regan, Tom, "McCloskey on Why Animals Cannot Have Rights," *Philosophical Quarterly*, Vol. 26, July, 1976.

Regan, Tom, "The Moral Basis of Vegetarianism," *The Canadian Journal of Philosophy*, Vol. 5, October, 1975.

Regan, Tom, "Narveson on Egoism and the Rights of Animals," *The Canadian Journal of Philosophy*, Vol. 7, March, 1977.

Regan, Tom, "On the Right to Be Spared Gratuitous Suffering," *Canadian Journal of Philosophy*, forthcoming.

Regan, Tom, "Utilitarianism, Vegetarianism and Animal Rights," *Philosophy and Public Affairs*, forthcoming.

Ritchie, A. M., "Can Animals See? A Cartesian Query," *Proceedings of the Aristotelian Society*, Vol. 64, 1963-64.

Rodman, John, "Animal Justice: The Counter-Revolution in Natural Right and Law," *Inquiry*, Vol. 22, Spring-Summer, 1979.

Rodman, John, "The Liberation of Nature?" *Inquiry*, Vol. 20, Spring, 1977. (A discussion of Peter Singer's *Animal Liberation* and Christopher Stone's *Should Trees Have Standing?*)

Salt, Henry S., "The Rights of Animals," *Ethics*, Vol. 10, No. 2, January, 1900, pp. 206-222.

Seidler, Michael J., "Hume and the Animals," *Southern Journal of Philosophy*, Vol. 15, Fall, 1977.

Singer, Peter, "All Animals Are Equal," *Philosophic Exchange*, Vol. 1, No. 5, Summer, 1974.

Singer, Peter, "The Fable of the Fox and the Unliberated Animals," *Ethics*, Vol. 88, January, 1978.

Singer, Peter, "Killing Humans and Killing Animals," *Inquiry*, Vol. 22, Spring-Summer, 1979.

Sprigge, T. L. S., "Metaphysics, Physicalism, and Animal Rights," *Inquiry*, Vol. 22, Spring-Summer, 1979.

Squadrito, Kathy, "Locke's View of Dominion," *Environmental Ethics*, Vol. 1, No. 3, Fall, 1979.

Squadrito, Kathy, "A Note Concerning Locke's View of Property Rights and The Rights of Animals," *Philosophia* (Israel), forthcoming.

Steinbock, Bonnie, "Speciesism and the Idea of Equality," *Philosophy*, Vol. 53, April, 1978.

Stich, Stephen P., "Do Animals Have Beliefs?" *Australasian Journal of Philosophy*, Vol. 57, March, 1979.

Sumner, L. W., "A Matter of Life and Death," *Nous*, Vol. 10, May, 1976.

Tranoy, Knut Erik, "Hume on Morals, Animals, and Men," *Journal of Philosophy*, Vol. 56, January, 1959.

VanDeVeer, Donald, "Animal Suffering," *Canadian Journal of Philosophy*, forthcoming.

VanDeVeer, Donald, "Interspecific Justice," *Inquiry*, Vol. 22, Spring-Summer, 1979.

Watson, Richard A., "Self-Consciousness and the Rights of Nonhuman Animals and Nature," *Environmental Ethics*, Vol. 1, Summer, 1979.

Weiss, Donald, "Professor Malcolm on Animal Intelligence," *Philosophical Review*, Vol. 84, January, 1975.

ESSAYS, SELECTIONS, ARTICLES, DISCUSSIONS, REVIEWS, ETC.

Aldrich, Thomas B., "The Cruelty of Science," in Aldrich, Thomas B., *Ponkapog Papers*, Essay Index Reprint Series, Books for Libraries Press, Freeport, New York, 1969.

Alexander, Samuel, "Mind of a Dog," in Alexander, Samuel, *Philosophical and Literary Pieces*, Macmillan Publishing Co., London, 1939, pp. 97–115. Also University Microfilms, Ann Arbor, Michigan, 1969.

Appleton, Tim, "Consciousness in Animals," *Zygon*, Vol. 11, December, 1976.

Armstrong, David M., "Belief and Language," in Armstrong, David M., *Belief, Truth and Knowledge*, University Press, Cambridge, 1973, pp. 24–37. (Discussion of whether animals have beliefs.)

Austin, Jack, "Buddhist Attitudes Towards Animal Life," in *Animals' Rights—A Symposium*, ed. by Richard D. Ryder and David Paterson, Centaur Press, London, 1979.

Axon, William E. A., "Shelley's Vegetarianism," Haskell House, Brooklyn, New York, 1971, 13 pp.

Balz, Albert G. A., "Cartesian Doctrine and the Animal Soul," in Balz, Albert G. A., *Cartesian*

Studies, Columbia University Press, New York, 1951.

Barr, James, "Man and Nature: The Ecological Controversy and the Old Testament," in *Ecology and Religion in History*, ed. by David and Eileen Spring, Harper & Row, New York, 1974.

Bayle, Pierre, "Rorarius," "Pereira," "Sennertus," in Bayle, Pierre, *Historical and Critical Dictionary: Selections*, ed. by Richard H. Popkin, The Bobbs-Merrill Co., Indianapolis, Indiana, 1965. (These articles contain comments on animals.)

Benson, J., "Hog in Sloth, Fox in Stealth: Man and Beast in Moral Thinking," in Royal Institute of Philosophy, *Nature and Conduct*, ed. by R. S. Peters, Macmillan Publishing Co., London, 1975, pp. 265-80.

Blackstone, William T., "The Search for an Environmental Ethic," in *Matters of Life and Death*, ed. by Tom Regan, Random House, New York, 1979.

Blake, Jeanie, "Animal Rights," *The Times-Picayune*, New Orleans, Louisiana, December 10, 1978.

Blake, Jeanie, "Man's Inhumanity," *The Times-Picayune*, New Orleans, Louisiana, December 3, 1978.

Blake, Jeanie, "Animal Rights and the Law," *The Times-Picayune*, New Orleans, Louisiana, December 17, 1978.

Boas, George, "Theriophily," in *Dictionary of the History of Ideas*, ed. by Philip P. Wiener, Vol. 4, Charles Scribner's Sons, New York, 1973.

Bradford, Nettie, "Property Rights of Animals," *Bulletin of University of Utah*, Vol. 37, No. 9, Salt Lake City, Utah, 1946.

Brinton, H. H., "Quakers and Animals," in Brinton, A. C., ed., *Then and Now*, University of Pennsylvania Press, Philadelphia, 1960.

Brophy, Brigid, "The Darwinist's Dilemma," in *Animals' Rights—A Symposium*, ed. by Richard D. Ryder and David Paterson, Centaur Press, London, 1979.

Brophy, Brigid, "In Pursuit of a Fantasy," in *Animals, Men and Morals*, ed. by Stanley and Roslind Godlovitch and John Harris, Gollancz, London, 1971; also Taplinger, New York, 1971. (On vivisection.)

Brophy, Brigid, "The Rights of Animals," *Sunday Times*, London, October 10, 1965. Reprinted by the Vegetarian Society (U.K.) Limited, Parkdale, Dunham Road, Altrincham, Cheshire, United Kingdom.

Brumbaugh, Robert S., "Of Man, Animals, and Morals: A Brief History," in *On the Fifth Day*, ed. by Richard Knowles Morris and Michael W. Fox, Acropolis Press, Washington, D.C., 1978.

Bryant, J. M., "Animal Exploitation in Human Recreation," in *Animals' Rights-A Symposium*, ed. by Richard D. Ryder and David Paterson, Centaur Press, London, 1979.

Burr, Stephen I., "Animal Experimentation: The British Point of View," *Animals*, Massachusetts Society for the Prevention of Cruelty to Animals, August, 1979.

Appendix

Burr, Stephen I., "Should Animals Have Legal Rights?" *Animals*, Massachusetts Society for the Prevention of Cruelty to Animals, July–August, 1977.

Burr, Stephen I., "Toward Legal Rights for Animals," *Environmental Affairs*, Boston College Law School, Vol. 4, No. 2, Spring, 1975.

Burroughs, John, "The Animal Mind," in Burroughs, John, *The Writings of John Burroughs: The Summit of the Years*, Houghton Mifflin Co., Boston, 1913.

Burroughs, John, "What Do Animals Know?" "Do Animals Think and Reflect?" in Burroughs, John, *Ways of Nature*, Essay Index Reprint Series, Books for Libraries Press, Freeport, New York, 1971.

Burton, Richard, "Our Elder Brothers," in Burton, Richard, *Little Essays in Literature and Life*, Century Co., New York, 1914.

Butler, Samuel, "Thought and Language," in Butler, Samuel, *The Humor of Homer and Other Essays*, Essay Index Reprint Series, Books for Libraries Press, Freeport, New York, 1967. (Discussion of thought and language in animals and man.)

Butler, Samuel, "The Views of an Erewhonian Prophet Concerning the Rights of Animals," and "The Views of an Erewhonian Philosopher Concerning the Rights of Vegetables," in Butler, Samuel, *Erewhon and Erewhon Revisited*, Modern Library, New York, 1955, chaps. 26 and 27.

Campbell, Clare; Worden, Alastair; and Ryder,

Richard, "Experiments on Animals: With a Review Discussion of *The Plague Dogs* by Richard Adams," *Theoria to Theory*, Vol. 12, April, 1978.

"Can Some Knowledge Simply Cost Too Much?" *The Hastings Center Report*, Vol. 5, No. 1, February, 1975, pp. 6–8. (A discussion generated by Frederick Wiseman's film *Primate*, with participation by Graham Shedd, Frederick Wiseman, Adrian Perachio, David Baltimore, Richard Lewontin, Robert Nozick.)

Caras, Roger, "Are We Right in Demanding an End to Animal Cruelty?" in *On the Fifth Day*, ed. by Richard Knowles Morris and Michael W. Fox, Acropolis Press, Washington, D.C., 1978.

Carrighar, Sally, *Wild Heritage*, Houghton Mifflin Co., Boston, 1965. (See pp. 135–182, "How Red the Tooth and Claw?"; also pp. 3–50, "Animals and Men: The Blurred Borderline.")

Carson, Hampton L., "The Trial of Animals and Insects: A Little-Known Chapter of Medieval Jurisprudence," *American Philosophical Society Proceedings*, Vol. 56, 1917, pp. 410–415.

Chesterton, Gilbert K., "Meaning of Mock Turkey," in Chesterton, Gilbert K., *Man Who Was Chesterton*, comp., and ed. by R. T. Bond, Dodd, Mead & Co., New York, 1937, pp. 71–79.

Clark, Stephen R. L., "How to Calculate the Greater Good," in *Animals' Rights—A Symposium*, ed. by Richard D. Ryder and David Paterson, Centaur Press, London, 1979.

Cobb, John B., Jr., "Beyond Anthropocentrism in

Appendix

Ethics and Religion," in *On the Fifth Day*, ed. by Richard Knowles Morris and Michael W. Fox, Acropolis Press, Washington, D.C., 1978.

Cobb, John B. Jr., "The Population Explosion and the Rights of the Subhuman World," IDOC International, North American ed., New York, 1970.

Curtis, Patricia, "New Debate Over Experimenting with Animals," *The New York Times Magazine*, December 31, 1978, pp. 18-23.

Curtis, Patricia, "Skeleton in the Laboratory Closet: Animal Experimentation," *Animals*, Massachussets Society for the Prevention of Cruelty to Animals, Boston, June, 1979.

Daggett, Herman, "The Rights of Animals," an oration delivered at Providence College, September 7, 1791. Reprinted by the American Society for the Prevention of Cruelty to Animals, 1926, 13 pp. (There is a copy of this in the University of Minnesota Library.)

Dallery, Carleton, "Thinking and Being with Beasts," in *On the Fifth Day*, ed. by Richard Knowles Morris and Michael W. Fox, Acropolis Press, Washington, D.C., 1978.

Darwin, Charles, "Comparison of the Mental Powers of Man and the Lower Animals," from *The Descent of Man*, Chaps. III and IV, Appleton and Co., New York, 1909. Reproduced in part in *Animal Rights and Human Obligations*, ed. by Tom Regan and Peter Singer, Prentice-Hall, Englewood Cliffs, New Jersey, 1976.

Deeley, John N., "Animal Intelligence and Concept-Formation," *Thomist*, Vol. 35, January, 1971, pp. 43–93.

Dennis, Clarence, "America's Littlewood Crisis: The Sentimental Threat to Animal Research," *Surgery*, Vol. 60, 1966, pp. 827–829.

Dichter, Anita, "Legal Definitions of Cruelty and Animal Rights," *Boston College Environmental Affairs Law Review*, Vol. 7, No. 1, 1978.

Dodgson, Charles, "Some Popular Fallacies About Vivisection," and "Vivisection as a Sign of the Times," in *The Works of Lewis Carroll*, Hamlyn Publishing, Middlesex, 1965, pp. 1089–1100.

Dowding, Muriel the Lady, "Furs and Cosmetics: Too High a Price?" in *Animals, Men and Morals*, ed. by Stanley and Roslind Godlovitch and John Harris, Gollancz, London, 1971; also Taplinger, New York, 1971.

Duffy, Maureen, "Beasts for Pleasure," in *Animals, Men and Morals*, ed. by Stanley and Roslind Godlovitch and John Harris, Gollancz, London, 1971; also Taplinger, New York, 1971. (Hunting, fishing, circus.)

Fallows, James, "Lo, the Poor Animals!" *Atlantic Monthly*, September, 1976.

Feinberg, Joel, "Human Duties and Animal Rights," in *On the Fifth Day*, ed. by Richard Knowles Morris and Michael W. Fox, Acropolis Press, Washington, D.C., 1978.

Feinberg, Joel, "The Rights of Animals and Unborn Generations," in *Philosophy and Environmental Crisis*, ed. by William Blackstone, University of Georgia Press, Athens, Georgia, 1974.

Flew, Anthony, "Torture: Could the End Justify the Means?" *Crucible*, January, 1974.

Fox, Michael A., "Animal Rights: Misconceived Humaneness," *Dalhousie Review*, Vol. 58, June, 1978.

Fox, Michael A., "The Use and Abuse of Animals," *Queen's Quarterly*, Vol. 83, No. 1, Spring, 1976, pp. 178-187.

Fox, Michael W., "From Animal Science to Animal Rights," in *Proceedings of First World Congress on Ethology Applied to Zootechnics*, Madrid, 1978.

Fox, Michael W., "Animal Rights and Nature Liberation," in *Animals' Rights—A Symposium*, ed. by Richard D. Ryder and David Paterson, Centaur Press, London, 1979.

Fox, Michael W., "Man and Nature: Biological Perspectives," in *On the Fifth Day*, ed. by Richard Knowles Morris and Michael W. Fox, Acropolis Press, Washington, D.C., 1978.

Fox, Michael W., "What Future for Man and Earth? Toward a Biospiritual Ethic," in *On the Fifth Day*, ed. by Richard Knowles Morris and Michael W. Fox, Acropolis Press, Washington, D.C., 1978.

Frankena, William K., "The Ethics of Respect for Life," in *Respect for Life in Medicine, Philosophy and the Law*, ed. by Stephen F. Barker, Johns Hopkins Press, Baltimore, Maryland, 1976.

Frazer, Sir James G., "Language of Animals," in Frazer, Sir James G., *Garnered Sheaves*, Books for Libraries Press, Freeport, New York, 1967.

French, Richard D., "Animal Experimentation:

Historical Aspects," *Encyclopedia of Bioethics*, Vol. 1, The Free Press, a Division of Macmillan Publishing Co., New York, 1978.

Frey, R. G., "What Has Sentiency to Do with the Possession of Rights?" in *Animals' Rights—A Symposium*, ed. by Richard D. Ryder and David Paterson, Centaur Press, London, 1979.

Friend, Charles E., "Animal Cruelty Laws: The Case for Reform," *University of Richmond Law Review*, Vol. 8, 1974, pp. 201, 216.

Galant, Debbie, "Animals Behind Bars," *Environmental Action*, Vol. 9, No. 17, January 14, 1978.

Galsworthy, John, "For Love of Beasts," "Reverie of a Sportsman," "The Slaughter of Animals for Food," "On Performing Animals," "Vivisection of Dogs," in Galsworthy, John, *A Sheaf*, William Heinemann, London, 1916.

Galton, Lawrence, "Pain Is Cruel, but Disease Is Cruel Too," *New York Times Magazine*, February 26, 1967, pp. 30-31.

Garrison, W. B., "Storm Center of Medical Research," in Garrison, Webb B., *Codfish, Cats, and Civilization*, Doubleday, Garden City, New York, 1959.

Geach, Peter, "Animal Pain," in Geach, Peter, *Providence and Evil*, Cambridge University Press, Cambridge, 1977.

Geison, Gerald L., "A Scientist's Dilemma in Historical Perspective: Pasteur's Work on Rabies: Reexamining the Ethical Issues," *Hastings Center Report*, Vol. 8, April, 1978, pp. 26-33.

Gill James E., "Theriophily in Antiquity: A Supplementary Account," *Journal of History of Ideas*, Vol. 30, July-September, 1969.

Glacken, Clarence J., *Traces on the Rhodian Shore: Nature and Culture in Western Thought from Ancient Times to the End of the Eighteenth Century*, University of California Press, Berkeley, California, 1967. (See especially "Interpreting Man's Dominion over Nature," pp. 295-302, "Animals—Wild and Domestic," pp. 309-311, "Hunting," pp. 346-347, "Count Buffon: On Domestications," pp. 672-679.)

Godlovitch, Roslind, "Animals and Morals," in *Animals, Men and Morals*, ed. by Stanley and Roslind Godlovitch and John Harris, Gollancz, London, 1971; also Taplinger, New York, 1971.

Godlovitch, Stanley, "Utilities" (using other beings), in *Animals, Men and Morals*, ed. by Stanley and Roslind Godlovitch and John Harris, Gollancz, London, 1971; also Taplinger, New York, 1971.

Gooch, G. B., "Curiosity in Wild Animals," in *Essays of the Year: 1929-1930*, Argonaut Press, London, 1930.

Hahn, Emily, "Getting Thru to the Others: Animal Communication," Part I: *New Yorker*, April 17, 1978; Part II: *New Yorker*, April 24, 1978.

Haldane, John B. S., "Some Enemies of Science," in *Possible Worlds and Other Essays*, Chatto & Windus, London, 1945.

Hanula, Robert W., and Hill, Peter Waverly, "Using Metaright Theory to Ascribe Kantian Rights to Animals within Nozick's Minimal State," *Arizona Law Review*, University of Arizona, Vol. 19, No. 1, 1977.

Harris, John, "Killing for Food," in *Animals, Men and Morals*, ed. by Stanley and Roslind Godlovitch and John Harris, Gollancz, London, 1971; also Taplinger, New York, 1971.

Harris, John, "Killing for Food," in *Animals' Rights—A Symposium*, ed. by Richard D. Ryder and David Paterson, Centaur Press, London, 1979.

Harrison, Ruth, "Ethical Questions Concerning Livestock Farming," in *Animals' Rights—A Symposium*, ed. by Richard D. Ryder and David Paterson, Centaur Press, London, 1979.

Harrison, Ruth, "On Factory Farming," in *Animals, Men and Morals*, ed. by Stanley and Roslind Godlovitch and John Harris, Gollancz, London, 1971; also Taplinger, New York, 1971.

Hart, H. L. A., "Are There Any Natural Rights?" in *Political Philosophy*, ed. by Anthony Quinton, Oxford University Press, London, 1967.

Hartshorne, Charles, *Born to Sing: An Interpretation and World Survey of Bird Song*, Indiana University Press, Bloomington, 1973. (See pp. 14–34, "Animal Music in General"; also pp. 35–57, "Bird Song Compared to Human Music.")

Hartshorne, Charles, "Foundations for a Humane Ethics: What Human Beings Have in Common with Other Higher Animals," in *On the Fifth Day*, ed. by Richard Knowles Morris and Michael W. Fox, Acropolis Press, Washington, D.C., 1978.

Hasker, William, "The Souls of Beasts and Men," *Religious Studies*, Vol. 10, September, 1974.

Hegarty, Terence, "Alternatives" (to experimenting on animals), in *Animals, Men and Morals*, ed. by Stanley and Roslind Godlovitch and John Harris, Gollancz, London, 1971; also Taplinger, New York, 1971.

Holmes, Samuel J., "Some Controverted Questions of Right and Wrong," in Holmes, Samuel J., *Life and Morals*, Macmillan Publishing Co., New York, 1948, pp. 144–75. (On animal experimentation.)

Hugo, Victor, "The Relationship Between Men and the Animals," *The Ark*, Journal of the Catholic Study Circle for Animal Welfare, August, 1969.

Hume, David, "Of the Reason of Animals," in *An Enquiry Concerning Human Understanding*, Sec. IX, in *Hume's Enquiries*, ed. by L. A. Selby-Bigge, Clarendon Press, Oxford, 1970.

Hume, David, *A Treatise of Human Nature*, ed. by L. A. Selby-Bigge, Clarendon Press, Oxford, 1960.
See:
"Of the Reason of Animals," Book I, Part III, Sec. XVI.
"Of the Pride and Humility of Animals," Book II, Part I, Sec. XII.

"Of the Love and Hatred of Animals," Book II, Part II, Sec. XII.

"Of Natural Abilities," Book III, Part III, Sec. IV, p. 610.

"Of Personal Identity," Book I, Part IV, Sec. VI, p. 253f.

"Of Our Esteem for the Rich and Powerful," Book II, Part II, Sec. V, p. 363.

"Of the Direct Passions," Book II, Part III, Sec. IX, p. 448.

"Moral Distinctions Not Derived from Reason," Book III, Part I, Sec. I, p. 468.

Hunt, Morton, "Man and Beast," in Montagu, Ashley, ed., *Man and Aggression*, Oxford University Press, New York, 1973.

Hyde, Walker W., "The Prosecution and Punishment of Animals and Lifeless Things in the Middle Ages and Modern Times," *University of Pennsylvania Law Review*, Vol. 64, p. 709.

Inge, William R., "Our Poor Relations," in Inge, William R., *Rustic Moralist*, Putnam, East Rutherford, New Jersey, 1937, pp. 313-317.

Inge, William R., "Rights of Animals," in Inge, William R., *Wit and Wisdom of Dean Inge*, Essay Index Reprint Series, Books for Libraries Press, Freeport, New York, 1968.

Jast, L. Stanley, "Why I Am Not a Vegetarian," in Jast, L. Stanley, *Libraries and Living*, Essay Index Reprint Series, Books for Libraries Press, Freeport, New York, 1969.

Jevons, William S., "Cruelty to Animals: A Study

in Sociology," in Jevons, William S., *Methods of Social Reform and Other Papers*, A. M. Kelley, New York, 1965.

Johnson, Samuel, *The Idler*, No. 17, Saturday (August 5, 1758) (attack on vivisection), in *The Yale Edition of Works of Samuel Johnson*, Vol. II, ed. by W. J. Bate, John M. Bullitt, and L. F. Powell, Yale University Press, New Haven, Connecticut, 1963.

Jones, R. K., "The Ethological Fallacy: A Note in Reply to Mr. Meynell," *Philosophy*, Vol. 47, January, 1972.

Kant, Immanuel, "Duties to Animals and Spirits," in his *Lectures on Ethics*, trans. by Louis Infield, Harper & Row, New York, 1963.

Koch, Carl Henrik, "Man's Duties to Animals: A Danish Contribution to the Discussion of Rights of Animals in the Eighteenth Century," *Danish Yearbook of Philosophy*, Vol. 13, 1976, pp. 11–28.

Koehler, Otto, "Animal Languages and Human Speech," in *The Human Creature*, ed. by Günter Altner, Anchor Press, Garden City, New York, 1969.

Krutch, Joseph Wood, *The Great Chain of Life*, Houghton Mifflin Co., Boston, 1977. (See "Reverence for Life," p. 147; also "Undeveloped Potentialities" (of animals), p. 129.)

Krutch, Joseph Wood, "Not as Dumb as You Think," in Krutch, Joseph Wood, *Best of Two Worlds*, Sloane, New York, 1953.

Langer, Susanne K., "Man and Animal: The City and the Hive," in Langer, Susanne K., *Philosophical Sketches*, Johns Hopkins Press, Baltimore, Maryland, 1962.

Lawler, J. G., "On the Rights of Animals," *Anglican Theological Review*, April, 1965.

Leach, Edmund, "Animal Categories and Verbal Abuse," *New Directions in the Study of Language*, ed. by Eric Lenneberg, MIT Press, Cambridge, Massachusetts, 1964.

Lee, Amy Freeman, "A Game for All Seasons," in *On the Fifth Day*, ed. by Richard Knowles Morris and Michael W. Fox, Acropolis Press, Washington, D.C., 1978. (Violence, hunting, trapping, rodeos, furs.)

Levin, Michael, "All in a Stew about Animals: A Reply to Singer," *Humanist*, Vol. 37, September-October, 1977.

Levin, Michael, "Animal Rights Evaluated," *Humanist*, Vol. 37, July-August, 1977.

Lewis, C. S., "Animal Pain," in Lewis, C. S., *The Problem of Pain*, Macmillan Publishing Co., New York, 1962.

Lewis, C. S., "Vivisection," in *God in the Dock*, Eerdmans Publishing, Grand Rapids, Michigan, 1970.

Lewis, C. S., and Joad, C. E. M., "The Pains of Animals," in *God in the Dock*, Eerdmans Publishing, Grand Rapids, Michigan, 1970. ("The Inquiry," by C. E. M. Joad, "The Reply," by C. S. Lewis.)

Appendix 203

Limburg, James, "What Does It Mean to 'Have Dominion over the Earth'?" *Dialog*, Summer, 1971, pp. 221-223.

Linzey, Andrew, "Animals and Moral Theology," in *Animals' Rights—A Symposium*, ed. by Richard Ryder and David Paterson, Centaur Press, London, 1979.

Loew, Franklin M., "The Veterinarian and Intensive Livestock Production: Humane Considerations," *Canadian Veterinarian Journal*, Vol. 13, No. 10, October, 1972.

Lovejoy, A. O., and Boas, George, *Primitivism and Related Ideas in Antiquity*, Octagon Books, Farrar, Straus & Giroux, New York, 1973. (See Chap. XIII: "The Superiority of Animals.")

Magel, Charles R., "A Bibliography on Animal Rights and Related Matters," forthcoming.

Magel, Charles R., "A Boundless Ethic Which Includes the Animals Also." Magel, Professor of Philosophy at Moorhead State University, interviewed by John Ydstie, Producer/Reporter, KCCM, Minnesota Public Radio, Concordia College, Moorhead, Minnesota. Available in the form of an 80-minute cassette tape; may be purchased from the Moorhead State University Philosophy Department, Moorhead, Minnesota, 56560.

Magel, Charles R., "Human Rights and Animal Rights," Society for Animal Rights, Clarks Summit, Pennsylvania, 1979.

Mayo, Charles W., "The Paradox of the Well-Intentioned Enemies of Medical Research," President's Address, read before the 71st Annual Session of the Western Surgical Association, Galveston, Texas, November 21-23, 1963, published in *Archives of Surgery*, April, 1964. Copies of this address are available from The American Anti-Vivisection Society, Philadelphia, Pennsylvania.

Meth, Theodore Sager, "Animal Rights," *Animals*, Massachusetts Society for the Prevention of Cruelty to Animals, Boston, Vol. 110, No. 6, November-December, 1977.

Montaigne, Michel de, "Man Is No Better than the Animals," in *Apology for Raymond Sebond* in *The Complete Works of Montaigne*, trans. by Donald M. Frame, Stanford University Press, Stanford, California, 1958, pp. 330-358. Also, see pp. 306-318, "Of Cruelty."

Morris, Clarence, "Rights and Duties of Beasts and Trees," *Journal of Legal Education*, Vol. 17, 1964-1965, pp. 185 ff.

Morris, Richard Knowles, "Man and Animals: Some Contemporary Problems," in *On the Fifth Day*, ed. by Richard Knowles Morris and Michael W. Fox, Acropolis Press, Washington, D.C., 1978.

Murphy, Earl Finbar, "Has Nature Any Right to Life?" *Hastings Law Journal*, Vol. 22, 1971.

Nelson, Leonard, "Duties to Animals," in Nelson, Leonard, *System of Ethics*, Yale University Press, New Haven, Connecticut, 1956, pp.

136-144. Also in *Animals, Men and Morals*, ed. by Stanley and Roslind Godlovitch and John Harris, Gollancz, London, 1971; also Taplinger, New York, 1971.

Nietzsche, Friedrich, *The Complete Works of Friedrich Nietzsche*, ed. by Oscar Levy, Russell & Russell, New York, 1964.

Vol. 5: *Schopenhauer as Educator*, No. 5, pp. 147-155. (Human pity for animals, the lot of the wild beasts.)

Vol. 7: *Human, All-Too-Human*, Part II, "The Wanderer and His Shadow," No. 57, "Intercourse with Animals," pp. 225-227.

Vol. 9, *The Dawn of Day*, No. 286, "Domestic Animals, Pets and the Like," p. 258.

Vol. 10: *The Joyful Wisdom*, No. 224, "Animal Criticism," p. 200.

Northrup, F. S. C., "Naturalistic Realism and Animate Compassion," in *On the Fifth Day*, ed. by Richard Knowles Morris and Michael W. Fox, Acropolis Press, Washington, D.C., 1978.

Nozick, Robert, "Constraints and Animals," in Nozick, Robert, *Anarchy, State and Utopia*, Basic Books, New York, 1974, pp. 35-51.

Otten, Jim, and Russow, Lilly-Marlene, "Forum: Experimentation on Animals," *Eros*, Department of Philosophy, Purdue University, West Lafayette, Indiana, 1977.

Paget, G. E., "The Ethics of Vivisection," *Theology*, July, 1975.

Peters, Michael, "Nature and Culture," in *Animals,*

Men and Morals, ed. by Stanley and Roslind Godlovitch and John Harris, Gollancz, London, 1971; also Taplinger, New York, 1971.

Plutarch, "The Cleverness of Animals," "Beasts Are Rational" (A dialogue between Odysseus, Circe, and Gryllus), "On the Eating of Flesh," in *Plutarch's Moralia*, trans. by Harold Cherniss and William Helmbold, Harvard University Press, Cambridge, Massachusetts, 1957, Vol. 12, Secs. 959-999.

Pope, Alexander, "Of Cruelty to Animals," in *Hundred English Essays*, ed. by Rosalind Valance, Nelson, Toronto, 1936, pp. 159-165. Also in Carver, George, ed. *Periodical Essays of the Eighteenth Century*, Essay Index Reprint Series, Books for Libraries Press, Freeport, New York, 1970.

Premack, D., "On Animal Intelligence," in *Perspectives on Intelligence*, ed. by H. Jerison, Appleton-Century-Crofts, New York, forthcoming.

Puka, Bill, A review of *Animal Liberation*, by Peter Singer, in *Philosophical Review*, Vol. 86, October, 1977.

Rachels, James, "Do Animals Have a Right to Liberty?" in *Animal Rights and Human Obligations*, ed. by Tom Regan and Peter Singer, Prentice-Hall, Englewood Cliffs, New Jersey, 1976.

Rachels, James, "A Reply to VanDeVeer," in *Animal Rights and Human Obligations*, ed. by Tom Regan and Peter Singer, Prentice-Hall, Englewood Cliffs, New Jersey, 1976.

Rachels, James, "Vegetarianism and 'The Other Weight Problem,' " in *World Hunger and Moral Obligations*, ed. by W. Aiken and H. LaFollette, Prentice-Hall, Englewood Cliffs, New Jersey, 1977.

Reed, T. J., "Nietzsche's Animals: Idea, Image and Influence," in *Nietzsche: Imagery and Thought*, ed. by Malcolm Pasley, University of California Press, Berkeley, California, 1978.

Regan, Tom, "Animals and the Law: The Need for Reform," *Proceedings of the World Congress on Philosophy of Law and Social Philosophy*, Basel, Switzerland, August, 1979.

Regan, Tom, "Exploring the Idea of Animal Rights," in *Animals' Rights—A Symposium*, Centaur Press, London, 1978.

Regan, Tom, A review of *The Moral Status of Animals*, by Stephen R. L. Clark, in *Philosophical Books*, Vol. 19, October, 1978.

Rensberger, Boyce, "Man and Beast," in Rensberger, Boyce, *The Cult of the Wild*, Doubleday, Garden City, New York, 1977.

Rensch, Bernhard, "Basic Aesthetic Principles in Man and Animals," in *The Human Creature*, ed. by Günter Altner, Anchor Press, Garden City, New York, 1969.

Rikleen, Lauren S., "The Animal Welfare Act: Still a Cruelty to Animals," *Boston College Environmental Affairs Law Review*, Vol. 7, No. 1, 1978.

Roberts, Catherine, "The Utilization of Animals

in Medical Research," and "Humanism and the Rhesus," in Roberts, Catherine, *The Scientific Conscience*, George Braziller, New York, 1967.

Roberts, Catherine and White, Robert J., "Animal Experimentation and Evolution," *The American Scholar*, Vol. 40, No, 3, Summer, 1971. (Two opposing views on vivisection.)

Rollin, Bernard E., "Beasts and Men: The Scope of Moral Concern," *The Modern Schoolman*, March, 1978.

Rollin, Bernard E., "Moral Philosophy and Veterinary Medical Education," *Journal of Veterinary Medical Education*, Fall, 1977.

Rollin, Bernard E., "Updating Veterinary Medical Ethics," *Journal of the American Veterinary Medical Association*, Vol. 173, No. 8, 1978.

Routley, Richard and Val, "Against the Inevitability of Human Chauvinism," in *Ethics and Problems of the 21st Century*, ed. by Kenneth E. Goodpaster and Kenneth M. Sayre, University of Notre Dame Press, Notre Dame, Indiana, 1979.

Rowan, Andrew N., "Alternatives to Laboratory Animals in Biomedical Programs," *Animal Regulation Studies*, Vol. 1, November, 1977, pp. 103–128.

Ryder, Richard, "Experiments on Animals," in *Animals, Men and Morals*, ed. by Godlovitch and Harris. Also in *Animal Rights and Human Obligations*, ed. by Tom Regan and Peter Singer.

Ryder, Richard, "The Struggle Against Specieism, "in *Animals' Rights—A Symposium*, ed. by Richard D. Ryder and David Paterson, Centaur Press, London, 1979.

Sagan, Carl, "The Abstractions of Beasts," in Sagan, Carl, *The Dragons of Eden*, Random House, New York, 1977.

Salisbury, David, "Research with Animals," *The Christian Science Monitor*, Boston, March 8, 9, and 10, 1978.

Salt, Henry S., "Logic of the Larder" and "The Humanities of Diet," from Salt, Henry S., *The Humanities of Diet*. Reproduced in *Animal Rights and Human Obligations*, ed. by Tom Regan and Peter Singer, Prentice-Hall, Englewood Cliffs, New Jersey, 1976.

Scheler, Max, "The Stages of Psychophysical Life in Plant, Animal and Man," in Scheler, Max, *Man's Place in Nature*, Beacon Press, Boston, 1961.

Schiller, Joseph, "Claude Bernard and Vivisection," *Journal of the History of Medicine*, Vol. 22, 1967, pp. 246-260.

Schweitzer, Albert, "The Ethics of Reverence for Life," and "The Civilizing Power of the Ethics of Reverence for Life," in Schweitzer, Albert, *The Philosophy of Civilization*, Part II, Macmillan Publishing Co., New York, 1960.

Schweitzer, Albert, "The Sacredness of All That Lives," in *Albert Schweitzer: An Anthology*, Harper & Bros., New York, 1947.

Sebeok, Thomas A., "Animals as Artists," *Animals,*

Massachusetts Society for the Prevention of Cruelty to Animals, August, 1979.

Sebeok, Thomas A., "Prefigurements of Art," *Semiotica*, Vol. 26, Nos. 3 and 4, 1979. (Artistic activities of animals.)

Sebeok, Thomas A., "Talking with Animals," *Animals*, Massachusetts Society for the Prevention of Cruelty to Animals, December, 1978.

Shaw, George Bernard, *The Doctor's Dilemma: A Tragedy*, in Shaw, Bernard, *Collected Plays with Their Prefaces*, The Bodley Head, London, 1971. (See the "Preface on Doctors" for an extended discussion of the medical profession and vivisection.)

Shaw, George B., "Man of Science," in Shaw, George B., *Everybody's Political What's What*, Dodd, Mead & Co., New York, 1944. (On animal experimentation.)

Shaw, George Bernard, "Killing for Sport," in Hamalian, L. and Volpe, E. L., eds., *Great Essays by Nobel Prize Winners*, ed. by L. Hamalian and E. L. Volpe, Farrar, Strauss & Giroux, New York, 1960.

Shelley, Percy B., "Essay on the Vegetable System of Diet," and "Vindication of Natural Diet," in *Shelley's Prose*, University of New Mexico Press, Albuquerque, New Mexico, 1954.

Singer, Isaac Bashevis.

A vegetarian, Nobel Prize winner Singer occasionally introduces the topics of vegetarianism, slaughtering of animals, flesh eating and man's

Appendix

treatment of animals into his novels and stories. For example (in *Enemies, A Love Story*, Farrar, Straus and Giroux, New York, 1972, p. 257): "As often as Herman had witnessed the slaughter of animals and fish, he always had the same thought: in their behavior toward creatures, all men were Nazis. The smugness with which man could do with other species as he pleased exemplified the most extreme racist theories, the principle that might is right." Another example (in "The Letter Writer," in Singer's *The Seance and Other Stories*, Farrar, Straus & Giroux, New York, 1968, p. 270): "In his thoughts, Herman spoke a eulogy for the mouse who had shared a portion of her life with him and who, because of him, had left this earth. 'What do they know—all these scholars, all these philosophers, all the leaders of the world—about such as you? They have convinced themselves that man, the worst transgressor of all the species, is the crown of creation. All other creatures were created merely to provide him with food, pelts, to be tormented, exterminated. In relation to them, all people are Nazis; for the animals it is an eternal Treblinka.'"
Also the short story "The Slaughterer" in *an Isaac Bashevis Singer Reader*, Farrar, Straus & Giroux, New York, 1977, pp. 219-234.
For a discussion of Singer's views on vegetarianism see Dudley Giehl's *Vegetarianism: A Way of Life*, Harper & Row, New York, 1979, pp. 141-145. Also see Singer's Foreword to this book.

Singer, Peter, "Animal Liberation," in *The New York Review of Books*, Vol. 20, No. 3, April 5, 1973. (A review of *Animals, Men and Morals*, ed. by Stanley and Roslind Godlovitch and John Harris.)

Singer, Peter, "Animal Experimentation: Philosophical Perspectives," *Encyclopedia of Bioethics*, Vol. 1, The Free Press, a Division of Macmillan Publishing Co., New York, 1978.

Singer, Peter, "Animals and the Value of Life," in *Matters of Life and Death*, ed. by Tom Regan, Random House, New York, 1979.

Singer, Peter, "The Morality of Experimenting with Animals," in *Philosophy and Science: The Wide Range of Interactions*, ed. by Frederick E. Mosedale, Prentice-Hall, Englewood Cliffs, New Jersey, 1979.

Singer, Peter, "Not for Humans Only: The Place for Nonhumans in Environmental Issues," in *Ethics and Problems of the 21st Century*, ed. by Kenneth E. Goodpaster and Kenneth M. Sayre, University of Notre Dame Press, Notre Dame, Indiana, 1979.

Singer, Peter, "A Reply to Professor Levin's 'Animal Rights Evaluated'," *Humanist*, Vol. 37, July-August, 1977.

Singer, Peter, "Value of Life," *Encyclopedia of Bioethics*, Vol. 2, The Free Press, a Division of Macmillan Publishing Co., New York, 1978.

Smith, David H., "Scientific Knowledge and Forbidden Truths: Are There Things We Should Not

Know?", *Hastings Center Report*, Vol. 8, December, 1978.

Sprigge, T. L. S., "The Animal Welfare Movement and the Foundations of Ethics," in *Animals' Rights—A Symposium*, ed. by Richard D. Ryder and David Paterson, Centaur Press, London, 1979.

Stevenson, Lloyd G., "Religious Elements in the Background of the British Anti-Vivisection Movement," *Yale Journal of Biology and Medicine*, Vol. 29, 1956, pp. 125–157.

Stewart, Desmond, "The Limits of Trooghaft," *Encounter*, London, February, 1972. Reproduced in *Animal Rights and Human Obligations*, ed. by Tom Regan and Peter Singer, Prentice-Hall, Englewood Cliffs, New Jersey, 1976.

Sumner, L. W., A review of *The Moral Status of Animals*, by Stephen R.L. Clark, in *Dialogue* (Canada), Vol. 17, 1978, pp. 570–575.

Swift, Jonathan, "A Modest Proposal for Preventing the Children of Poor People from Being a Burthen to Their Parents or Country and for Making Them Beneficial to the Public," 1729. Reproduced in *Animal Rights and Human Obligations*, ed. by Tom Regan and Peter Singer, Prentice-Hall, Englewood Cliffs, New Jersey, 1976. (Satiric argument that roast pork is no more defensible than roast children.)

Thomas Aquinas, Saint, "Differences Between Rational and Other Creatures," in *Summa*

Contra Gentiles, Third Book, Part II, Chap. CXII. Reproduced in *Animal Rights and Human Obligations*, ed. by Tom Regan and Peter Singer, Prentice-Hall, Englewood Cliffs, New Jersey, 1976.

Thomas Aquinas, Saint, "On Killing Living Things and the Duty to Love Irrational Creatures," from *Summa Theologia*, Part II, Question 64, Art. 1, and Question 25, Art. 3. Reproduced in *Animal Rights and Human Obligations*, ed. by Tom Regan and Peter Singer, Prentice-Hall, Englewood Cliffs, New Jersey, 1976.

Thomason, Sir John A., "Do Animals Think?, in Thomson, Sir John A., *Riddles of Science*, Essay Index Reprint Series, Books for Libraries Press, Freeport, New York, 1971.

Tolstoy, Leo, "The First Step," in Tolstoy, Leo, *Recollections and Essays*, Oxford University Press, London, 1961. (This essay, written in 1892, served as a preface to a Russian translation of Howard Williams' *The Ethics of Diet*. It includes descriptions of his visits to slaughterhouses and stresses the immorality of eating animal flesh.)

Townsend, Aubrey, A review of *The Moral Status of Animals*, by Stephen R. L. Clark, and of *Animal Liberation*, by Peter Singer, in *Australasian Journal of Philosophy*, Vol. 57, March, 1979.

Twain, Mark, "Man's Place in the Animal World," in *The Works of Mark Twain*, Vol. 19, *What Is Man? And Other Philosophical Writings*, ed. by Paul Baender, University of California Press, Berkeley, California, 1973, pp. 80–89.

VanDeVeer, Donald, "Defending Animals by Appeal to Rights," in *Animal Rights and Human Obligations*, ed. by Tom Regan and Peter Singer, Prentice-Hall, Englewood Cliffs, New Jersey, 1976.
Visscher, Maurice B., "Medical Research and Ethics," *Journal of the American Medical Association*, Vol. 199, No. 9, Feb. 27, 1967.
" Vivisection-Vivistudy: The Facts and the Benefits to Animal and Human Health," *American Journal of Public Health*, Vol. 57, 1967, pp. 1597–1626. (Four papers presented at a symposium of medical and veterinary specialists.)
Voltaire, François M. A. de, "Beasts," in Voltaire, François M. A. de, *Philosophical Dictionary*, trans. by Peter Gay, Basic Books, New York, 1962. Reproduced in *Animal Rights and Human Obligations*, ed. by Tom Regan and Peter Singer, Prentice-Hall, Englewood Cliffs, New Jersey, 1976.
Wagner, Richard, "Against Vivisection," in Wagner, Richard, *Richard Wagner's Prose Works*, Vol. 6, trans. by William A. Ellis, Broude Brothers, New York, 1966, pp. 195–210.
Weber, Shierry M., "Vegetarianism: The Experience of Praxis," in *Critical Interruptions*, ed. by Paul Breines, Herder and Herder, New York, 1970, pp. 55–59.
Wellbourn, F. B., "Man's Dominion," *Theology*, Vol. 78, 1975, pp. 561 ff.
Westermarck, Edward A., "Christianity and the Regard for the Lower Animals," in Westermarck,

Edward A., *Christianity and Morals*, Macmillan, Publishing Co., New York, 1939, pp. 379–393.

Westermarck, Edward, "Regard for Lower Animals," in Westermarck, Edward, *The Origin and Development of Moral Ideas*, Vol. 2, Macmillan, Publishing Co., London, 1926, pp. 490–514.

White, Lynn, "Continuing the Conversation," in *Western Man and Environmental Ethics*, ed. by Ian G. Barbour, Addison-Wesley, Reading, Massachusetts, 1973. (A critique of those Animal Liberationists who try simply to extend utilitarianism to include non-humans.)

White, Lynn, "The Historical Roots of Our Ecologic Crisis," *Science*, Vol. 155, March, 10, 1967. Also in Spring, David and Eileen, eds., *Ecology and Religion in History*, ed. by David and Eileen Spring, Harper & Row, New York, 1974, Prentice-Hall, Englewood Cliffs, New Jersey, 1976.

White, Robert J., "Antivivisection: The Reluctant Hydra," *The American Scholar*, Vol. 40, No. 3, Summer, 1971. Reproduced in *Animal Rights and Human Obligations*, ed. by Tom Regan and Peter Singer.

Wickler, Wolfgang, "Group Ties in Animals and Man," in *The Human Creature*, ed. by Günter Altner, Anchor Press, Garden City, New York, 1969.

Appendix

Wiseman, Fred, prod., *Meat*, 16-mm film, 2 hours, available through television station WNET, 356 West 58th St., New York, N. Y. 10019. (Powerful portrayal of meat-packing operation.)

Wisemen, Fred, prod., *Primate*, 16-mm film, 105 minutes, available from Zipporah Films, 54 Lewis Wharf, Boston, Massachusetts, 02110. (Controversial film of the Yerkes Primate Research Center, Atlanta, Georgia.)

Wood, David, "Strategies," in *Animals, Men and Morals*, ed. by Stanley and Roslind Godlovitch and John Harris, Gollancz, London, 1971; also Taplinger, New York, 1971. (Social and individual delusional mechanisms used by humans in indefensible treatment of animals.)

Wrighton, Basil, "The Moral and Religious Aspects of Vivisection," National Anti-Vivisection Society, London, 1959.

Wye, Charles, "Toward a New Ethic: A Humanitarian Philosophy with Special Reference to Man's Relationship to Animals," Philosophical Society of England, 82 Lavington Road, London W 13, 1957.

Wynne-Tyson, Jon, "Dietethics: Its Influence on Future Farming Patterns," in *Animals' Rights–A Symposium*, ed. by Richard D. Ryder and David Paterson, Centaur Press, London, 1979.

Ydstie, John, prod., "The Rights of Animals," 50-minute taped discussion broadcast July 15, 1978. Participants: Charles Magel, Professor of Philosophy, Moorhead State University; Tom Morse, Manager, Fargo Beef Industries, West Fargo, North Dakota; William Beatty, Professor of Psychology, North Dakota State University. Cassette available from KCCM, Minnesota Public Radio, Box 72, Concordia College, Moorhead, Minnesota 56560.

WORKS BY HENRY S. SALT

A *Group of Unpublished Letters by Henry S. Salt to Joseph Ishill with an Appreciation by Henry W. Nevinson*, Oriole Press, Berkeley Heights, New Jersey, 1942.

A *Plea for Vegetarianism and Other Essays*, Vegetarian Society, Manchester, 1886.

A *Shelley Primer*, Reeves and Turner, London, 1887; Kennikat Press Corp., Port Washington, New York, 1969; AMS Press, Inc., New York, 1975.

A *Study of Shelley's "Julian and Maddale' to Which Is Added a Note on the Identification of 'The Aziola' by H. T. Wharton*, Richard Clay & Sons, London, 1888.

An Examination of Hogg's 'Life of Shelley,' Richard Clay & Sons, London, 1889.

Animals' Rights Considered in Relation to Social Progress, George Bell & Sons, Ltd., London; Macmillan Publishing Co., New York, 1892; Macmillan Publishing Co., New York, 1894; The Humanitarian League, London, 1899; A. C. Fifield, London, 1899; A. C. Fifield, London, 1905, The Humanitarian League, London, 1915; George Bell & Sons, Ltd., London, 1922; Society for Animal Rights, Inc., Clarks Summit, Pennsylvania, 1980.

Company I Have Kept, George Allen & Unwin, London, 1940.

Consolations of a Faddist, Verses Reprinted from 'The Humanitarian,' A. C. Fifield, London, 1906.

Cum Grano, Verses and Epigrams, Oriole Press, Berkeley Heights, New Jersey, 1931.

"David Henry Thoreau: A Centenary Essay," The Humanitarian League, London, 1917.

De Quincey, George Bell & Sons, Ltd., London; Macmillan, New York, 1904; Folcroft Library Editions, Folcroft, Pennsylvania, 1978.

Edward Carpenter's Writings, E. W. Allen, London, 1891.

Eton under Hornby: Some Reminiscences and Reflections, A. C. Fifield, London, 1910.

"Fallacies of Flagellants," The Humanitarian League, London, 1913.

"Flesh or Fruit? An Essay on Food Reform," Reeves and Turner, London, 1888.

Humanitarianism: Its General Principles and Progress, Reeves and Turner, London, 1891; Reeves and Turner, London, 1893; The Humanitarian League, 1906, Watts and Co., London, 1926.

Life of Henry David Thoreau, Richard Bentley & Son, London, 1890; Walter Scott, Ltd., London, 1896; Charles Scribner's Sons, New York, 1896; Archon Books, Hamden, Connecticut, 1968.

Literae Humaniores, An Appeal to Teachers, The Humanitarian League, London, 1891.

Literary Sketches, Swan, Sonnenschein, Lowrey & Co., London, 1886 and 1888.

Appendix

Memories of Bygone Eton, Hutchinson & Co., London, 1928.

On Cambrian and Cumbrian Hills: Pilgrimages to Snowdon and Scawfell, A. C. Fifield, London, 1908; A. C. Fifield, London, 1911; C. W. Daniel, London, 1922.

Our Vanishing Wildflowers and Other Essays, with an Afterword by Sir Maurice Abbot-Anderson, Watts and Co., London, 1928.

Percy Bysshe Shelley, Swan, Sonnenscheim, Lowrey & Co., London, 1888 and 1892.

Percy Bysshe Shelley: Poet and Pioneer, Reeves and Turner, London, 1896; Charles Scribner's Sons, New York, 1896; A. C. Fifield, London, 1905; Watts and Co., London, 1913; George Allen & Unwin, London, 1924; Kennikat Press Corp., Port Washington, New York, 1968.

Richard Jeffries: A Study, Swan, Sonnenscheim, Lowrey & Co., London, 1893; Macmillan Publishing Co., New York, 1894; A. C. Fifield, London, 1905; A. C. Fifield, London, 1913.

Seventy Years among Savages, George Allen & Unwin, London, 1921; T. Seltzer, Inc., New York, 1921.

Shelley as a Pioneer of Humanitarianism, The Humanitarian League, London, 1902.

Shelley's Principles: Has Time Refuted or Confirmed Them: A Retrospect and Forecast, Reeves and Turner, London, 1892; Haskell House Publishers, Ltd., Brooklyn, New York, 1977.

"Socialism and Literature," in *Forecasts of the*

Coming Century, Labour Press Society, Manchester, 1897.

Tennyson As a Thinker, Reeves and Turner, London, 1893, A. C. Fifield, 1909, Folcroft Library Editions, Folcroft, Pennsylvania, 1977.

"The Case against Corporal Punishment," The Humanitarian League, London, 1913.

The Creed of Kinship, Constable & Co., London, and E. P. Dutton & Co., New York, 1935.

"The Ethics of Corporal Punishment," The Humanitarian League, London, 1907 and 1909.

The Eton Hare Hunt, A. C. Fifield, London, 1909.

"The Faith of Richard Jeffries," Watts and Co., London, 1906.

The Flogging Craze: A Statement of the Case Against Corporal Punishment, with a Foreword by Sir George Greenwood, George Allen & Unwin, London, 1916.

The Heart of Socialism: Letters to a Public School Man, with a Preface by Lord Olivier, Independent Labour Party, London, 1928.

The Humanities of Diet, Some Reasonings and Rhymings, The Humanitarian League, London, 1897; The Vegetarian Society, Manchester, 1914.

The Life of James Thomson ('B. V.') with a Selection from His Writings and a Study of His Writings, Reeves and Turner, London, 1889; A. & H. B. Bonner, London, 1898; A. C. Fifield, London, 1905; Watts and Co., London, 1914.

The Logic of Vegetarianism: Essays and Dialogues, Ideal Publishing Union, Ltd., London, 1899; George Bell & Sons, Ltd., London, 1906; George

Appendix

Bell & Sons, Ltd., London, 1918; London Vegetarian Society, London, 1932 and 1933.

The New Charter, A Discussion of the Rights of Men and the Rights of Animals, address delivered before the Humanitarian League, George Bell & Sons, Ltd., London, 1896.

The Nursery of Toryism: Reminiscences and Reflections, A. C. Fifield, London, 1911.

The Secret of the Reptile House: Snake Feeding at the Zoological Gardens, The Humanitarian League, London, 1909.

The Song of the Respectables and Other Verses, Labour Press Society, Manchester, 1896.

"The Sportsman at Bay," The Humanitarian League, London, 1906.

The Story of My Cousins, Watts and Co., London, 1922 and 1935.

"Thoreau and the Simple Life," in *Humane Review*, v. 7, January, 1907, London.

Two Similar Pastimes: Sport and War, second edition, reprinted from *The Creed of Kinship*, National Society for the Abolition of Cruel Sports, London, 1947.

WORKS EDITED BY HENRY S. SALT

A Vindication of Natural Diet, by Percy Bysshe Shelley, F. Pitman, London; J. Heywood and the Vegetarian Society, Manchester, 1884.

Anti-Slavery and Reform Papers, by Henry David Thoreau, Swan, Sonnenscheim, Lowrey & Co., London, 1890.

Cruelties of Civilization: A Program of Humane Reform, Reeves and Turner, London, 1895 and 1897.

Godwin's 'Political Justice,' A Reprint of the Essay on 'Property' from the Original Edition, Swan, Sonnenscheim, Lowrey & Co., London, 1890.

Hand and Brain: A Symposium of Essays on Socialism, Roycrofters, Aurora, New York, 1898.

Killing for Sport: Essays by Various Writers, with a Preface by George Bernard Shaw, George Bell & Sons, Ltd., London, 1914 and 1917.

Kith and Kin: Poems of Animal Life, George Bell & Sons, Ltd., London, 1901.

Poems of Nature, by Henry David Thoreau, edited by Henry S. Salt and Frank H. Sanborn, John Land, London; Houghton Mifflin & Co., New York and Boston, 1895.

Political Justice: A Reprint of the Essay on Property from the Original Edition by William Godwin, George Allen & Unwin, London, 1929.

Selected Works of Shelley, Watts and Co., London, 1912.

Songs of Freedom, W. Scott, Ltd., London and New York, 1893.

Songs of the Army of the Night, by Francis Adams, with an Introduction by Henry S. Salt, 1894.

The Story of Dido and Aeneas: The Fourth Book of Virgil's 'Aeneid,' Translated into English Verse, Watts and Co., London, 1926: The University Press, Cambridge, 1928.

Appendix

Treasures Of Lucretius: Selected Passages from the 'De Rerum Natura,' Translated into English Verse by Henry S. Salt, Watts and Co., London, 1912.

BIOGRAPHICAL NOTES

HENRY S. SALT studied the writings of Thoreau throughout most of his life. He shared Thoreau's belief in vegetarianism and pacifism. He believed, as Thoreau did, that reformers should live simply, for the less money one needed, the freer one was to work for a better society. And Salt's writings, as was the case with Thoreau's, were read by few during his lifetime.

Salt, who was to have a great influence on Gandhi, was born in India in 1851, the son of Colonel T. H. Salt of the Royal Bengal Artillery. When Henry was a year old, his mother and he sailed to England where he spent a happy childhood in Shrewsbury. After being educated at Eton, where he spent the happiest years of his life, and Cambridge, he was offered a teaching position at Eton which he accepted.

In 1879, Salt married Catherine Leigh Joynes. Through the efforts of his brother-in-law, J. L. Joynes, Jr., Salt became acquainted with some of the leading social reformers of his day. Salt numbered among his friends and acquaintences George Bernard Shaw, Edward Carpenter, Henry George and William Morris.

Appendix

In 1884, Salt gave up his teaching position at Eton. The Salts had resolved to lead a simpler life. They set up housekeeping in a cottage near Tilford. Salt began writing for *Justice*, the journal of the Social Democratic Federation.

In 1886, Salt's *A Plea for Vegetarianism* was published. It was read by Gandhi when he was a student in London, and, as Gandhi later wrote in his autobiography, "From the date of reading this book, I may claim to have become a vegetarian by choice."

On September 10, 1890, Gandhi was elected to the executive committee on the London Vegetarian Society, and in May of 1891, both Gandhi and Salt attended the Conference of the Vegetarian Union. On the second day of this conference, both Gandhi and Salt presented papers.

Years later, in 1929, responding to a letter from Salt, Gandhi commented on the effect *A Plea for Vegetarianism* had had on his life: "Yes, indeed your book which was the first English book I had come across on vegetarianism was of immense help to me in steadying my faith in vegetarianism."

In 1889, Salt completed his excellent *Life of Henry David Thoreau*. This book, too, was to be read by Gandhi. And in 1890 Salt edited Thoreau's *Anti-Slavery and Reform Papers*, adding his own Introduction.

Salt and several of his friends in 1891 formed the Humanitarian League. The League published two journals: *Humanity* and *The Humanitarian*. Salt edited both.

The Humanitarian League was, in the truest sense, an animal rights organization. Salt and his friends were concerned with social justice in the broadest possible sense. The League opposed vivisection and hunting and encouraged vegetarianism. The League worked for prison reform and opposed the flogging of children—a practice which was common in schools of the time. Last of all, worthy of the heritage of Thoreau, the League encouraged pacifism and civil disobedience.

In 1892, George Bell & Sons published Salt's *Animals' Rights* in England. One of Salt's supporters, a Miss Eddy of Providence, Rhode Island, paid for an American edition of the book to be distributed free to libraries in the United States.

Salt edited *Selections from Thoreau* in 1895. Salt's purpose in editing this work was to make British readers aware of the importance of Thoreau's thought. In the same year, Salt and F. B. Sanborn edited Thoreau's *Poems of Nature*.

In 1919, Salt's first wife died, and in 1927 Salt married his housekeeper, Catherine Mandeville.

Salt wrote several autobiographies. *Seventy Years Among Savages*, published in 1921, spans the years in Salt's life between 1851 and 1921, *The Story of My Cousins*, published in 1923, deals with the animals who shared Salt's life. Salt's final autobiography, *Company I Have Kept*, was published in 1930.

On November 20, 1931, Gandhi delivered a speech at the London Vegetarian Society. Salt was present. Gandhi's opening remarks were as follows:

When I received the invitation to be present

Appendix

at this meeting, I need not tell you how pleased I was, because it revived old memories and recollections of pleasant friendships formed with vegetarians. I feel especially honored on my right, Mr. Henry Salt. It was Mr. Salt's book, *A Plea for Vegetarianism*, which showed me why, apart from hereditary habit, and apart from my adherence to a vow administered to me by my mother, it was right to be a vegetarian. He showed me why it was a moral duty incumbent on vegetarians not to live upon fellow-animals. It is, therefore, a matter of additional pleasure to me that I find Mr. Salt in our midst.

Henry Salt died in Brighton, England on April 19, 1939. He had prepared an address which was read at the burial service by his friend Bertram Lloyd. Part of the address was as follows:

Names are very liable to be misunderstood; and when I say that I shall die, as I have lived, a rationalist, socialist, pacifist and humanitarian, I must make my meaning clear. I wholly disbelieve in the present established religion; but I have a very firm religious faith of my own—a Creed of Kinship, I call it—a belief that in years yet to come there will be a recognition of the brotherhood between man and man, nation and nation, human and sub-human, which will transform a state of semi-savagery, as we have it, into one of civilization, when there will be no such barbarity as warfare, or the robbery of the poor by the rich, or the ill-usage of the lower animals by man.

The Creed of Kinship was understood by few during Salt's lifetime. Today, the full realization of Salt's vision is the goal of the animal rights movement.

PETER SINGER is Professor of Philosophy at Monash University, Victoria, Australia. He is the author of *Animal Liberation* and co-editor, with Tom Regan, of *Animal Rights and Human Obligations*. More recently he has worked with James Mason on *Animal Factories*, an illustrated book on factory farming. He has also written for the *New York Review of Books*, *The New York Times* and other popular publications.

"I first became aware," he has written, "of the prejudice that I, in common with most others, had against taking seriously the interests of animals when I was a student at Oxford. It was at this time that I met others who were vegetarians because of their concern for animals, and after making myself acquainted with the facts of our treatment of animals, I decided that there was no way in which the present situation could be justified ethically. I therefore became a vegetarian and began the research that has culminated in *Animal Liberation*."

CHARLES R. MAGEL is Professor of Philosophy at Moorhead State University, Moorhead, Minnesota. He was born in Burlington, Iowa, and received his doctorate in philosophy from the University of Minnesota in 1960.

Professor Magel has taught at St. Olaf College and

Appendix

the University of Minnesota. He has given four classes at Moorhead State University entitled "Animal Liberation."

Professor Magel participated in the Harlan Klintworth Memorial Symposium on Animal Experimentation in Laboratories in Madison, Wisconsin on May 12, 1979. He delivered an address, "Human Rights and Animal Rights," to the American Humane Association Annual Meeting in Miami, Florida on November 28, 1978. (Copies of this address are available from Society for Animal Rights.)

Along with Tom Regan, who is professor of philosophy at North Carolina State University, Professor Magel prepared a "Select Bibliography on Animal Rights and Human Obligations," which was published in the Summer, 1979 edition of *Inquiry*.

On November 8, 1979, Professor Magel delivered three lectures on the topic "Animal Rights" at St. Cloud State University, St. Cloud, Minnesota. He also delivered a lecture on the topic "Animals and Morals" at the University of Minnesota on January 15, 1980.

Professor Magel has prepared an extensive forthcoming *Bibliography on Animal Rights and Related Matters*.

Notes

Notes

Notes

Notes

Notes

Notes

Notes

Notes